COOL BOOK

JSIF

Emily C Saul

Rachel Shea

Rachel S

oh my Gaad oh my Gaad!
Someones lying on the
floor would you like
some cooffee,

MACMILLAN
MUSIC and YOU

Erin ♥'s
___

I will tell you something
for it - but <u>not</u>
<u>now!</u>

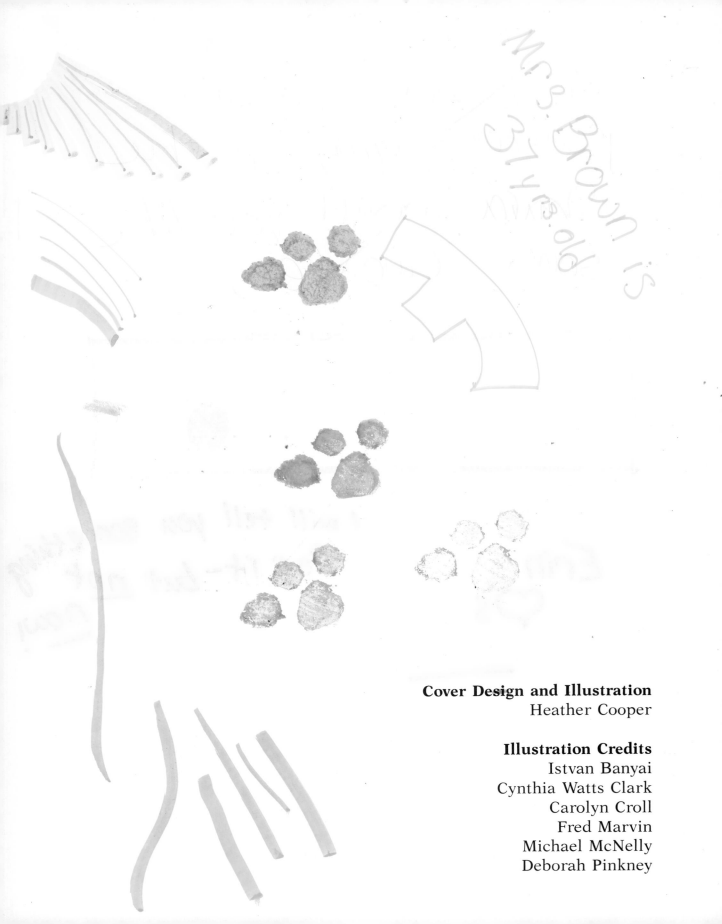

Cover Design and Illustration
Heather Cooper

Illustration Credits
Istvan Banyai
Cynthia Watts Clark
Carolyn Croll
Fred Marvin
Michael McNelly
Deborah Pinkney

MACMILLAN
MUSIC and YOU

Barbara Staton
Merrill Staton
Vincent Lawrence
Michael Jothen
Jeanne Knorr, Contributing Author

Macmillan Publishing Company
New York

Collier Macmillan Publishers
London

ACKNOWLEDGMENTS

Grateful acknowledgment is given to the following authors and publishers. In the case of songs and poems for which acknowledgment is not given, we have earnestly endeavored to find the original source and to procure permission for their use, but without success. Extensive research failed to locate the author and/or copyright holder.

Beckenhorst Press Inc. for the music to "Over the Sea to Skye" by Robert Louis Stevenson, arranged by Michael Jothen. Copyright © 1985 by Beckenhorst Press, Inc. All rights reserved. Used by permission; "Praise to the Lord" by Michael Jothen. Copyright © 1979 by Beckenhorst Press Inc. All rights reserved. Used by permission.

Boosey & Hawkes Inc. for *Lieutenant Kijé Suite* by Sergei Prokofiev. Used by permission of Boosey & Hawkes, Inc., publisher and copyright owner.

Columbia Pictures Publications for "Love Song" from *Pippin*, by Stephen Schwartz. Copyright © 1972 by Stephen Schwartz. All publishing, performance, exploitation rights for the world owned exclusively by Jobete Music Co., Inc. & Belwin-Mills Publishing Corporation and administered by Jobete Music Co. Inc. except in the United Kingdom, where administered by Belwin-Mills Music Ltd. I-M-A; "Dream a Dream," words and music by Ed Robertson. Copyright © 1977 by Studio 224, 224 South Lebanon Street, Lebanon, Indiana 46052. All Rights Reserved. International Copyrights Secured. Printed in U.S.A.; "To the Morning" by Dan Fogelberg. Copyright © 1975 by APRIL MUSIC INC. and HICKORY GROVE MUSIC. ADMINISTERED BY APRIL MUSIC INC. All rights of April Music Inc. assigned to SBK Catalogue Partnership. All rights controlled and administered by SBK APRIL Catalogue.

Dunvagen Music Publishing, Inc. for "Floe" from *Glassworks*, by Philip Glass. Copyright © 1982 Dunvagen Music Publishing, Inc. Reprinted by permission. All rights reserved.

Mark Foster Music Co. for "Hanerot Halalu" composed by Baruch J. Cohen, arranged by Blanche Chass, 1961. Used by permission of Mark Foster Music Company.

Harper & Row Publishers, Inc. for "Backward Bill" and illustration from A LIGHT IN THE ATTIC, by Shel Silverstein. Copyright © 1981 by Snake Eye Music, Inc.

Henry Holt and Co. for "Bravado," by Robert Frost. Copyright © 1947, © 1969 by Holt, Rinehart and Winston, Inc. Copyright © 1975 by Lesley Frost Ballantine, Reprinted from THE POETRY OF ROBERT FROST edited by Edward Connery Lathem, by permission of Henry Holt and Co., Inc.

Jenson Publications Inc. for "Our World" music by Lana Walter, words by Jane Foster Knox. Copyright © 1985 Jenson Publications, Inc. International Copyright Secured. Made in U.S.A. All rights reserved; "Winter Carol" by Mark Wilson and Jane Foster Knox. Copyright © 1980 by Jenson Publications, Inc. International Copyright Secured. Made in U.S.A. All rights reserved. Used by permission.

Julie Music Corp. for "Mi Caballo Blanco," by Francisco Flores del Campo. Copyright © 1971 by Julie Music Corp. All rights reserved. Used by permission.

Kodaly Center of America for "I'm Goin' Home on a Cloud" arranged by Sean Diebler, 1981. Copyright KCA Choral Series published by Kodaly Center of America.

Mineral River Music for "River," by Bill Staines from IF I WERE A WORD, THEN I'D BE A SONG. Copyright © 1977 Mineral River Music.

Moose Music Ltd. for "The Wreck of the Edmund Fitzgerald," by Gordon Lightfoot. Copyright © 1976 Moose Music Inc. Used by permission.

Music Sales Corp. for "Un bel dì vedremo" from MADAMA BUTTERFLY by Puccini, libretto by Giuseppe Giacosa and Lorenzo Illica. Used by arrangement with G. Schirmer, Inc., U.S. agent for G. Ricordi.

The New Music Company for "Radiator Lions" by Michael Jothen and Dorothy Aldis, reprinted and set to music by permission of G.P. Putnam's Sons from EVERYTHING AND ANYTHING by Dorothy Aldis. Copyright © 1925-1927, © renewed 1953-1955 by Dorothy Aldis. Music copyright © 1987 by The New Music Co. Used by permission. All rights reserved; "This Is Christmas" by Keith W. Derrickson and Jane Foster Knox. Copyright © 1987 by The New Music Co. Used by permission. All rights reserved.

Carl J. Nygard, Jr. for "The Promised Land," "Sing Me Home," and "Chichester Prayer." Copyright © 1986 by Carl J. Nygard, Jr. All rights reserved.

Random House, Inc. for "Dreams" by Langston Hughes, from THE DREAM KEEPER AND OTHER POEMS by Langston Hughes. Copyright © 1932 by Alfred A. Knopf, Inc. and renewed 1960 by Langston Hughes. Reprinted by permission of Alfred A. Knopf, Inc.

Marian Reiner for "Rainbow Writing" by Eve Merriam, from RAINBOW WRITING by Eve Merriam. Copyright © 1976 by Eve Merriam. All rights reserved. Reprinted by permission of Marian Reiner for the author.

G. Schirmer, Inc. for "Tonight" quintet from WEST SIDE STORY by Leonard Bernstein and Stephen Sondheim. Copyright © 1957 by Leonard Bernstein and Stephen Sondheim. All rights reserved. Used by arrangement with G. Schirmer, Inc.

Shawnee Press, Inc. for "The Ghost Ship" from REFLECTIONS OF A LAD AT SEA by Don Besig and Nancy Price. Copyright © 1982 by Shawnee Press, Inc., Delaware Water Gap, PA 18327. All Rights Reserved. Used with permission; "The Rhythm of Life" by Cy Coleman,

Macmillan Publishing Company
866 Third Avenue
New York, N.Y. 10022
Collier Macmillan Canada, Inc.

Printed in the United States of America

ISBN: 0-02-293450-2
9 8 7 6 5 4

AUTHORS

Barbara Staton has taught music at all levels, kindergarten through college, and for eight years was music television teacher for the State of Georgia. She is author of a four-volume series of books and records designed to teach music concepts through movement. She holds a B. S. degree in Music Education and an M. A. in Dance and Related Arts. Mrs. Staton has written numerous songs for television and recordings and is a composer member of ASCAP.

Dr. Merrill Staton earned his M. A. and Ed. D. degrees from Teachers College, Columbia University, and is nationally known as a music educator, choral conductor, singer, composer and record producer. He has been music director and has conducted the Merrill Staton Voices on many network TV series and recordings. Dr. Staton has been a leader in the field of music education for the past twenty-five years, and pioneered the use of children's voices on recordings for education.

Dr. Vincent Lawrence received his Ph.D. from Case Western Reserve University. He is currently Professor of Music at Towson State University in Maryland, where he is Chairperson of the Division of Music Education and directs the University Chorale. Dr. Lawrence has taught general and choral music in the Baltimore County public schools.

He has also served as a conductor, adjudicator, and clinician on national, state, and local levels.

Dr. Michael Jothen is currently Supervisor of Secondary Vocal and General Music for the Baltimore County public schools, Baltimore, Maryland. He is widely published as a choral composer, and has conducted choral clinics throughout the United States. His teaching experience includes work at the University of Northern Colorado and at Ohio State University. He has also taught vocal and general music in the public schools of Michigan and Ohio.

Jeanne Knorr teaches music education and theory at Towson State University in Maryland, and is pursuing her Ph.D. She has taught vocal and instrumental music at all levels. Ms. Knorr holds a Dalcroze-Orff-Kodaly Certificate from the Manhattan School of Music and a Dalcroze Certificate from the Longy School of Music.

SPECIAL CONTRIBUTORS

Dr. Betty Atterbury
Mainstreaming

Alex Campbell
Choral Music

Mary Frances Early
Black American Music

Dr. JaFran Jones
Ethnomusicology

CONSULTANTS AND CONTRIBUTING WRITERS

Dr. Clifford Alper, Towson State University, Towson, Maryland ● **Dr. James Anthony,** Towson State University, Towson, Maryland ● **Dr. Betty Atterbury,** University of Maine, Gorham, Maine ● **Teri Burdette,** Barnsley Elementary, Rockville, Maryland ● **Alex Campbell,** Jefferson County Schools, Golden, Colorado ● **Gregory Clouspy,** Franklin Senior High, Reisterstown, Maryland ● **Ruth Landis Drucker,** Towson State University, Towson, Maryland ● **Dr. Robert A. Duke,** University of Texas, Austin, Texas ● **Mary Frances Early,** Atlanta Public Schools, Atlanta, Georgia ● **Nancy Ferguson,** University of Arizona, Tucson, Arizona ● **Donna Brink Fox,** Eastman School of Music, Rochester, New York ● **Dr. Judith A. Jellison,** University of Texas, Austin, Texas ● **Dr. JaFran Jones,** Bowling Green State University, Bowling Green, Ohio ● **Jeanne Knorr,** Towson State University, Towson, Maryland ● **Tom Kosmala,** Music Supervisor, Pittsburgh Public Schools, Pittsburgh, Pennsylvania ● **Carl J. Nygard, Jr.,** Fleetwood Area Schools, Fleetwood, Pennsylvania ● **Jane Pippart,** West Chester University, West Chester, Pennsylvania ● **Cynthia Stephens,** Patapsco Middle School, Ellicott City, Maryland ● **Mollie Tower,** Austin Independent School District, Austin, Texas ● **José A. Villarrubia,** Towson State University, Towson, Maryland

contents

unit 1

*Exploring
Musical Styles* *1*

Introduction to Style 2
Style Makes the Difference................................ 6
Calypso Style 10
A Style from the Far East 12
The European-Western Styles 16
Baroque Style.. 18
Major and Minor in Two Styles 24
Synth-Pop: A Style of Rock Music........................ 30
Review 36

unit 2

*Rhythm Plays
a Role* *38*

Duple, Triple, and Quadruple Meter....................... 40
A Stage Style 44
Irregular Meter 48
A Jazz Style 52
Review 56

unit 3

*Rhythm Sets
the Beat*.. *58*

Compound Meter.. 60
A Song from *Cats* 62
Conducting in Compound Meter 66
Performing Polyrhythms.................................... 70
Review 74

unit 4

Melody **76**
Melody and Harmony 78
Texture in Music 82
A New Way to Organize a Melody 87
A New Kind of Pitch Organization 90
Review 94

unit 5

Harmony **96**
Changing Keys 98
The Blues—An American Style 104
Types of Harmony 108
Telling a Story Through Melody and Harmony 111
Review 116

unit 6

Form and Style **118**
Building Blocks of Form 120
Phrases of Different Lengths 123
Repetition: The Basis of Form 126
Story Through Song 130
Review 136

unit 7

Elements of Form **138**
Repetition in Music 140
Repetition and Development 146
Program Music 152
Creativity in the Twentieth Century 156
Review 160

unit 8

Tone Color in Different Styles 162

New Sounds 164
Perform with New Tone Colors 169
From Pipe Organ to Synthesizer 172
New Sounds from a Familiar Instrument 175
The Electronic Revolution 178
Recycling for Sound 181
Review 184

Year-End Review 186

Western Musical Styles 188

Music of the World's Cultures 208

Keyboards of Today 232

Playing the Guitar 254

Choral Singing 278

Time Line 361
Glossary 364
Listening Selections 368
Alphabetical Song Index 370
Classified Index 371

UNIT 1

EXPLORING MUSICAL STYLES

Detail from *The Ghent Altarpiece*, Jan van Eyck, CATHEDRAL OF ST. BAVON, Ghent

Figure of Horn Player (Benin bronze, Nigeria), Courtesy of MUSEUM OF PRIMITIVE ART, NY

INTRODUCTION TO STYLE

Musical styles differ throughout the world. Every composer hopes that his or her style will be distinctive. Music from different countries has different sounds. Listening to a variety of music can help you identify the source.

- As you listen, follow the pictures on pages x and 1 that represent the musical selections in "Style Montage."

 "Style Montage"

A Caribbean Style

- Listen to "Elements" by Black Uhuru (ōō-hōō′ rōō). Use illustrations on pages 2 and 3 to help you describe the musical characteristics of the selection.

 "Elements," by Black Uhuru

percussion instruments   voices in chorus

strong beat   weak beat

- Tap the steady **quarter note** (♩) beat with your foot and clap the rhythm pattern as you listen to "Elements" again. Make a silent palms-up motion on each **quarter rest** (𝄽). The **repeat signs** (‖: :‖) mean play the pattern again.

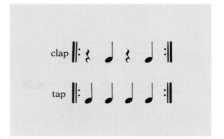

"Elements" has two different melodies. Call them A and B. Each time the A or B melody is played it is primarily vocal or instrumental.

- Follow the chart as you listen to the music one more time. Decide what should replace each question mark. How different is A′ (A-prime) from A?

	1.	2.	3.	4.	5.	6.	7.	8.	9.	10.
	Introduction	A	B	?	?	?	A′	?	?	Coda (Conclusion)
Mostly Vocal or Instrumental	I	V	V	?	?	?	I	?	?	I

solo   voices with instruments   accent

3

- Play this melody on a keyboard instrument or recorder. Each **half note** (♩) sounds as long as two quarter notes. Each **whole note** (o) sounds as long as four quarter notes.

E   D   D   C   C   D

- Play these chords on a keyboard instrument. A **chord** consists of three or more pitches sounding together. To play **G♯ (G-sharp)** on the keyboard, find the black key to the right of G.

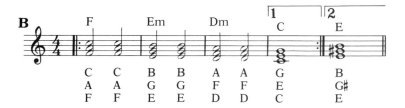

B	F		Em		Dm		C	E
	C	C	B	B	A	A	G	B
	A	A	G	G	F	F	E	G♯
	F	F	E	E	D	D	C	E

- Listen to "Elements" again. Play the melody above during the A section and the chords during the B section.

These photos show some popular reggae artists. On this page are scenes of Black Uhuru in performance.

Reggae

"Elements" is an example of a style of music called **reggae** (reʹ gā) that developed during the 1960s on the island of Jamaica in the Caribbean. Reggae music is very popular throughout the Caribbean islands, and its popularity has gradually spread to the United States and other parts of the world.

Reggae grew out of *ska* music, a fast, lively musical style that featured the trumpet, trombone, and saxophone. Ska was popular in Jamaica during the early 1960s. However, musical tastes and performances gradually changed. Songs became slower, rhythms became catchier, and a rhythm section of guitar, bass guitar, and drums replaced the brass instruments. The first song to mention this unique style of music by name was "Do the Reggay," recorded by Toots and the Maytals in 1968.

Early reggae music featured scratchy rhythm guitars, booming bass guitars, and a slow beat. Trumpets, trombones, and saxophones could still be heard on some recordings, and piano and organ were often used to fill out the sound. Hundreds of songs were written and recorded at this time in Kingston, the capital of Jamaica.

Recently, *dub* poetry has flourished in Jamaica and has made an impact in the United States and England. Dub consists of rhythmically spoken political poems "dubbed" over a reggae background, in a style similar to rap music. Dub poetry has rapidly become a way of expressing national pride in Caribbean countries.

Left, the reggae group Aswad. Above, Bob Marley, perhaps the most famous reggae artist, in performance.

STYLE MAKES THE DIFFERENCE

- Listen to *Bwala,* a dance from Uganda, and the Kyrie (kir′ ē-ā) from the Mass in G Minor by Ralph Vaughan Williams. What characteristics of each composition might help you identify its origin?

Bwala (dance from Uganda)
Kyrie from Mass in G Minor, by Ralph Vaughan Williams

In different cultures many things vary. The people may speak different languages. The foods they eat and the clothes they wear also may be different. The art and architecture produced by different cultures also have their own unique characteristics.

Detail from *Sir Osbert Sitwell,* Frank Dobson, THE TATE GALLERY, London

Wooden Mask, Songe tribe, Zaire

The sculpture on the left is by a twentieth-century English artist. The sculpture on the right is by an artist of the Songe tribe in Zaire. Although they both have the same subject, their styles are quite different.

Music from different times and cultures sounds different. The **style** of a culture is a unique mixture of its characteristics. The style of a musical composition is the unique mixture of its musical and cultural characteristics.

In *African Sanctus*, a new musical style results from combining the musical characteristics of different cultures. *Bwala* with its percussion, strong steady beat, and accents is combined with the choral singing tradition of Western cultures.

- Listen to *African Sanctus*. As each number is called, decide whether the music sounds more African or more Western. In which sections is it hard to make a choice?

 African Sanctus, by David Fanshawe

The style of *African Sanctus* is unique. The musical characteristics of two cultures have been combined to create music in a new style.
- Tap the steady quarter-note beat played on the drum as you listen to the opening choral part of *African Sanctus*. Then tap the following patterns as you listen again. Make a palms-up, silent motion for each quarter rest.

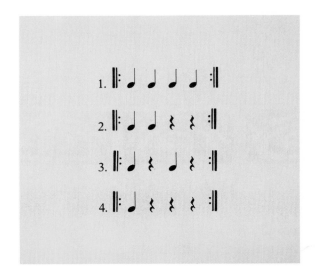

Each quarter note can be divided into two **eighth notes** (♪♪).

- Listen again to the opening choral section of *African Sanctus*, and clap two eighth-note sounds for each beat. As you clap, count aloud from 1 to 8, giving each clap one count.
- Listen to the second and third sections of *African Sanctus*. Clap and count the eighth notes in these sections. Is the new **tempo,** or speed of the beat, faster or slower than that of the first section?
- Listen to the complete *African Sanctus*. Perform these patterns with the choral sections by clapping and counting each line. Make the silent, palms-up motion for the **eighth rest** (𝄾).

- Select percussion instruments and play the patterns above as an accompaniment to *African Sanctus*.

 CHALLENGE   Create your own patterns to accompany *African Sanctus*.

Left, drummers at a festival in Vuaben, Ghana. Above, celebration at a baby-naming ceremony in Accra, Ghana. Below, South African women perform a mine dance.

CALYPSO STYLE

"Run Joe" is a **calypso** song about two brothers who get into trouble. Calypso texts are usually witty, making fun of political and economic issues. The music is rhythmic, danceable, and cheerful. It achieves its unique lilt by stressing melodic notes just ahead of or just behind the steady beat. This type of off-the-beat rhythm is called **syncopation.** Calypso music evolved in Trinidad, in the West Indies, toward the end of the nineteenth century. It also exhibits a strong African influence.

Run Joe

Words and music by Dr. Walt Merrick,
Joe Willoughby, and Louis Jordan

2. When you get home, you get to bed
   Call a doctor and tie your head.
   Can't tell Ma to invent a lie.
   Got to have a good alibi.

3. When the Judge ask me how I plea
   Not guilty, sir, most decidedly.
   You can see, judge, at a glance
   I'm the victim of circumstance.

4. If the judge believe what I say
   I'll be home by the break of day.
   If he don't, I'll be looking cute
   Behind the bars in my striped suit.

5. Mother told me not long ago
   Keep away from that worthless Joe.
   If I heard what my mama say
   Wouldn't be in this mess today.

- Perform this pattern during the verses of the song.

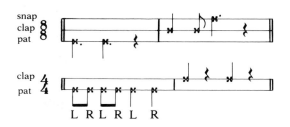

- Perform this pattern during the refrain. Pat your lap with your right and left hands.

You can accompany the refrain of "Run Joe" on guitar or keyboard using two chords built on G, the first (I), and D, the fifth (V), pitches of the **G major scale.**

The G or I chord is called the **tonic** chord and is built on the most important pitch or tone of this scale, the **key tone** or home tone. The D or V chord is built on the fifth pitch of this scale and is called the **dominant** chord.

- Listen to the refrain of "Run Joe." Place your palms down on your desk when you hear the I chord. Turn your palms upward when you hear the V chord.

The lowest pitch of each of these chords is called the **root.**

- Give the letter names of the roots of the I and V chords.
- Play the root of each chord on keyboard as you sing the refrain.
- Play the chords (I and V) as you sing the refrain.
- Play this pattern on bells or keyboard as you sing the refrain.

CHALLENGE Create your own melodic pattern on keyboard, bells, or recorder to play on the word *Joe* as you sing the refrain. Use these five pitches. Play your accompaniment as you sing the song.

G   A   B   D   E

A STYLE FROM THE FAR EAST

Satto (sä′ tō) or "Wind Dance" by Katsutoshi Nagasawa
(kät′ sōō-tō-shē nä′ gä-sä-wä) was composed for the theater in 1975
to suggest the feeling of the ancient Japanese spirit of the wind.

- Listen to *Satto*. You will hear several Japanese instruments.
  Decide how sound is produced on each of the instruments.

Satto, by Katsutoshi Nagasawa

These photos show
Japanese instruments,
flutes (above) and
drums (right).

A procession crossing a river at a Japanese festival

• Listen again and tap the steady beat. Is the tempo slow, moderate, or fast?

Contrast in *Satto* is achieved by the use of different *tone colors* and *dynamic* changes.

Tone color refers to the sound of the different instruments used. **Dynamics** are the levels of loudness and softness in music. They are shown by the abbreviations of the Italian words *piano* (p) for soft and *forte* (f) for loud.

To show gradual changes from one dynamic level to another, symbols and words are used.

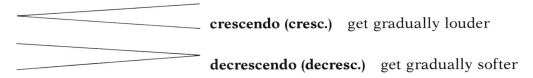

crescendo (cresc.)   get gradually louder

decrescendo (decresc.)   get gradually softer

• Listen to *Satto* once again to identify the dynamic changes. Clap the steady beat lightly when the music is loud. Tap the beat on the back of your hand when the music is soft.

Create a Sound Composition

Composers often get ideas from other art forms such as theater or poetry. You, too, will have the opportunity to be a composer and create a sound composition based on one of these poems.

- Read the poems aloud. Select one of them and create an original composition that will make a sound picture of the poem. Decide what tone colors, dynamics, and tempo you will use.
- Practice and perform your composition. Have other students guess which poem inspired your composition.

Rainbow Writing

Nasturtiums with
their orange cries
flare like trumpets;
their music dies.

Golden harps
of butterflies;
the strings are mute
in autumn skies.

Vermilion chords,
then silent gray;
the last notes of
the song of day.

Rainbow colors
fade from sight,
come back to me
when I write.

—*Eve Merriam*

Dreams

Hold fast to dreams
For if dreams die
Life is a broken-winged bird
That cannot fly.

Hold fast to dreams
For when dreams go
Life is a barren field
Frozen with snow.

—Langston Hughes

Bravado

Have I not walked without an upward look
Of caution under stars that very well
Might not have missed me when they shot and fell?
It was a risk I had to take—and took.

—Robert Frost

THE EUROPEAN-WESTERN STYLES

Symphony No. 9 by the German composer Ludwig van Beethoven (lōōd′ vig vän bā′ tō-ven) contains one of the most famous melodies ever written, the "Ode to Joy."

- Listen to the "Historical Style Montage." It first presents the "Ode to Joy" as Beethoven used it in his Symphony No. 9 and then as it might have sounded if used by composers who lived as much as four hundred years before Beethoven, or as much as one hundred fifty years after.

  How is each performance different? Think about tone color, instruments, dynamics, and tempo to help you decide.

 "Historical Style Montage"

- Perform the "Ode to Joy" on keyboard, bells, or recorder as you listen to the "Historical Style Montage." Begin after the Beethoven example.

"Ode to Joy" from Symphony No. 9, Fourth Movement

Ludwig van Beethoven

Each time you performed the "Ode to Joy," it was in a different musical style. In European-Western music the terms *Renaissance, baroque, classical, romantic,* and *twentieth century* are used to describe each of the musical styles.

Renaissance   Both religious and secular music, predominantly vocal, instruments used in secular music

Baroque   Steady rhythm, organ used to accompany religious music, secular music written for small groups

Classical   Short, tuneful melodies, gradual dynamic changes, restrained expression of emotions

Romantic   Longer, often complex melodies, more open expression of emotions

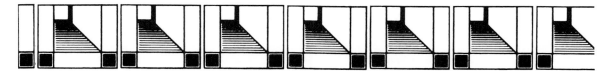

Twentieth Century   Unusual rhythms, emphasis on unusual tone colors, great emphasis on experimentation

• Listen to the "Historical Style Montage" again. Identify the order in which the style periods are presented. Use the musical descriptions above to explain your choices.

BAROQUE STYLE

Conducting a Baroque Composition

"Marche" by Jean Baptiste Lully (zhän′ bäp-tēst′ lyōō-lē′) has sections in different **meters,** or groupings of beats. Beats grouped in twos are **duple meter.** Beats grouped in threes are in **triple meter.** Groups of beats are shown in **measures** that are separated by **bar lines.**

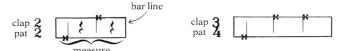

These are the conducting patterns for duple and triple meter. The photographs show the patterns when the conductor faces you.

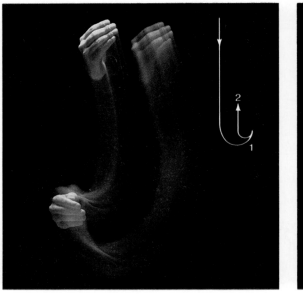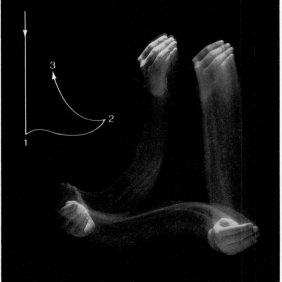

- Listen to the excerpt from Lully's "Marche." It has A and B sections. Tell which conducting pattern to use for each section. Describe the contrast in tempo between the two sections.

 "Marche" (excerpt) by Jean Baptiste Lully

- Listen to the entire "Marche" and conduct showing duple and triple meter.

 "Marche" by Jean Baptiste Lully

Jean Baptiste Lully

Jean Baptiste Lully (1632–1697) became King Louis XIV's most important and influential composer, producing operas and ballets to entertain the French court. For fifteen years Lully controlled much of the music performed in Paris. He was so popular that he was able to persuade King Louis XIV to force other composers to move away from Paris. Thus Lully managed to eliminate most of his competition. He earned enormous sums of money, but no amount ever seemed enough.

An unusual accident caused Lully's death. Instead of using a baton, conductors in those days often kept the steady beat by tapping a large stick on the floor. While conducting this way, Lully struck his own foot. An infection developed, which resulted in his death a month later.

During his career Lully wrote a great deal of dance music. His interest in orchestral tone color can be seen in the wide range of instruments he used in his works.

Analyzing a Baroque Composition

- Listen to Lully's "Marche" again and follow the map by pointing to each measure when the music is provided. When no music is shown, point to the pictures that represent the meter, tone color, dynamics, and form. At call number 4, **ritardando** (ri-tär-dän' dō) means a gradual slowing down of the tempo. At call number 9, the **coda** is the concluding section.

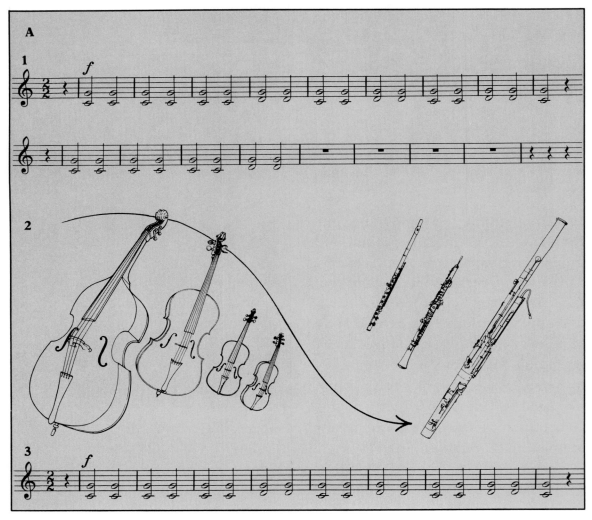

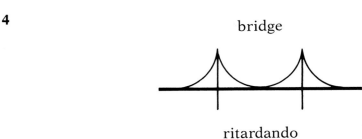

bridge

ritardando

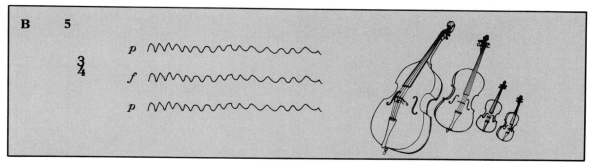

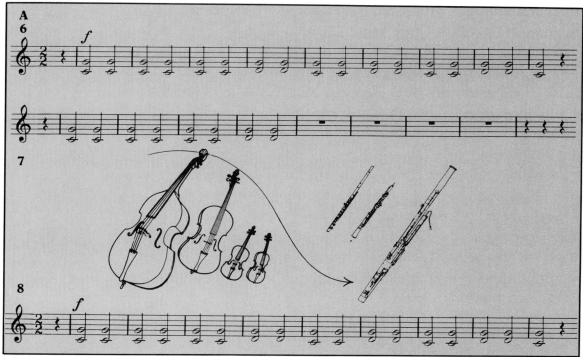

Repetition after a contrasting section creates an ABA, or ternary, form. **Ternary** means having three parts.

- Describe the contrasts between the A and B sections of Lully's "Marche." Identify contrasts in meter, tempo, and tone color.

- Play the A section and the coda of the "Marche" on recorder or keyboard.

The Baroque Period (1600–1750)

Royalty, wealthy families, and large churches hired composers of the baroque period to provide music for special occasions or for entertainment. Operas, ballets, and instrumental compositions were written for the world at large. Large religious choral works— Masses and cantatas—were composed for use in churches. For contrasts in tone color composers used a wide variety of instruments such as the organ, violin, flute, oboe, trumpet, and harpsichord.

Most baroque music has steady, rhythmic patterns. Each section of a larger composition conveys a single mood or emotion. Improvements in instruments made more complex music possible. Two of the most famous composers of all time, Johann Sebastian Bach (yō' hän se-bäs' tē-än bäкн') and George Frederick Handel (hän' del) lived during this period and produced some of the finest examples of baroque music.

Staircase at the Residenz (with frescos by Tiepolo), Würzburg

During the baroque period, elaborate styles of architecture, art, and clothing were popular. The exterior scene is of a palace in Vienna, Austria. The interior scene is in Würzburg, West Germany. The musicians in the painting are gathered for a formal portrait.

The Concert, Antonio Domenico Gabbiani

Characteristics of Baroque Music

Steady rhythms

Single mood in each section of a musical composition

Wide variety of instruments used for contrasts in tone color and dynamics

The Belvedere, Vienna

23

MAJOR AND MINOR IN TWO STYLES

A Romantic Composition

"Farandole" (fä-rän-dôl') is the final selection in the second *L'Arlésienne* (lär-lā-zē-en') Suite by the French romantic composer Georges Bizet (zhorzh' bē-zā'). A **suite** consists of several individual forms linked together. Bizet wrote the suite as background music for a play called *L'Arlésienne,* or "The Woman of Arles." You may recognize the first of the two themes as the Christmas carol "The March of the Three Kings."

• Listen to "Farandole." Each time you hear a number decide whether you are hearing Theme A or Theme B.

 "Farandole" from *L'Arlésienne* Suite No. 2, by Georges Bizet

GEORGES BIZET

Georges Bizet (1838–1875), great opera composer, was born in Paris into a family of professional musicians. His father and uncle were singing teachers, and his mother was an excellent pianist. Bizet showed great promise as a musician at an early age. He entered the Paris Conservatory at nine. At nineteen he had won several prizes for piano, organ, and composition.

Although Bizet was a brilliant pianist, his main interest was composing, especially opera. *Carmen* is his best-known work. His music is very melodic with simple orchestral accompaniments. His music for the play *L'Arlésienne* was ignored by the public when it was first presented in 1872. It was not appreciated until the play was revived after his death.

Theme A of "Farandole" begins with the D minor chord. Theme B begins with the D major chord.

D major chord   D minor chord

To play F# (F sharp) on the keyboard, find the black key to the right of F. The symbol ♮ is called a **natural**. It tells you to play F rather than F#. Changing this middle pitch from F# to F changes the D major chord to a D minor chord.

- Play the D minor and D major chords one after the other on keyboard, bells, or guitar to hear the difference between minor and major.

Bizet uses changes between major and minor, and changes in dynamics, to create the romantic style in "Farandole."

- Listen to "Farandole" again. In each section identify the use of major or minor, and changes in dynamics.

Arles, a city in southern France, was founded almost twenty-five hundred years ago. Many of its ancient buildings have been preserved.

25

The Romantic Period (1830–1900)

Much of the music in movies and on television can be traced back to the kind of music written in the nineteenth-century romantic period. Romantic artists and musicians tried to express their feelings, their outlook, and their hopes and dreams openly. Composers wrote instrumental works that told a story without words. Music became more descriptive, with changes in moods occurring within sections. Long, complex melodies were used to express these moods or emotions. As orchestras became larger and improved instruments were added, tone color became more important than it had been in earlier periods.

Left, the Opéra, Paris, built 1861–75

Music of the romantic period is very popular today. Many famous romantic works have been used as background music for extremely successful motion pictures. Some of the best known composers of this period were Ludwig van Beethoven (bā′ tō-ven), Franz Schubert (sho͞o′ bert), Robert Schumann (sho͞o′ män), Hector Berlioz (ber′ lē-ōz), Frédéric Chopin (shō′ pan), Richard Wagner (väg′ ner), Giuseppe Verdi (ver′ dē), Johannes Brahms (bräms′), Peter Ilyich Tchaikovsky (chī-käv′ skē), and Nicolai Rimsky-Korsakov (rim′ skē kor′ sä-kôv).

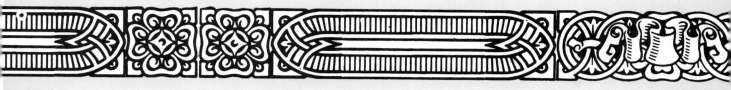

Florentine Story-teller, Vincenzo Cabianca, MUSEO DELL'ARTE MODERNA, Florence

The Ball, James Tissot, MUSÉE D'ORSAY, Paris

Characteristics of Romantic Music

Changes of mood within
sections of a composition

Direct expression of emotions

Long, often complex melodies

Use of large orchestra

Artists of the romantic
period often depicted
scenes of earlier times.
Top, an imaginary scene of
medieval Italy.
Right, women's fashions in
the nineteenth century
often were quite elaborate.

A Song in Major and Minor

"Our World" is a twentieth-century song that has sections in both major and minor.

- Listen to the repeated and contrasting sections. You will hear the A section repeat before you hear the B section. Which section is in major and which is in minor?
- Sing the song. Be sure to emphasize the contrasting sections.

Our World

Words by Jane Foster Knox
Music by Lana Walter

28

29

SYNTH-POP: A STYLE OF ROCK MUSIC

Synth-pop is a style of rock music in which the principal instrument is the synthesizer. **Synthesizers** are electronic keyboards that use computer technology to imitate the tone color of just about any musical instrument, or group of instruments. Often a drum machine provides the steady beat.

The synth-pop style first developed in England. It has a cool, shimmering tone color that is very different from the sound of guitar-based bands. Players in many synth-pop bands have had little formal musical training. Instead, they learned a few basic chords on the synthesizer and immediately began composing songs.

Depeche Mode (right and below) is a synth-pop group. Notice the synthesizer racks in the photograph below.

In the matched grip, both drumsticks are held in the same position.

- Practice these patterns with your drumsticks, using the percussion **matched grip.** When you see a quarter rest or an eighth rest, play silently in the air. Stress, or emphasize, the accented notes (♩).

- Find these patterns in the percussion score to "Head over Heels" on page 33.

- Play the rhythm accompaniment to "Head over Heels" on page 33. The symbol ⊢——2——⊣ in the score means that you should listen and count for two measures before continuing to play.

 "Head over Heels," by Curt Smith and Roland Orzabal

Below, Roland Orzabal (left) and Curt Smith (right). Right and bottom, Tears for Fears in performance

Head Over Heels
Rhythm Accompaniment

● Listen once more to "Head over Heels." Sing along with the recording and play a rhythmic accompaniment for the composition.

HEAD OVER HEELS

Words and music
by Roland Orzabal
and Curt Smith

1. I wanted to be with you alone
   And talk about the weather
   But traditions I can trace against the child in your face
   Won't escape my attention.
   You keep your distance with a system of touch
   And gentle persuasion.
   I'm lost in admiration could I need you this much?
   Oh you're just wasting my time,
        you're just just just wasting time.

REFRAIN
Something happens and I'm head over heels;
I never find out till I'm head over heels
Something happens and I'm head over heels;
Ah, don't take my heart, don't break my heart don't don't don't
        throw it away. (*First time only*: Throw it away, throw it away.)

2. I made a fire and watching it burn
   Thought of your future
   With one foot in the past now just how long will it last
   No, no, no have you no ambition
   My mother and my brothers used to breathing clean air
   And dreaming I'm a doctor
   It's hard to be a man when there's a gun in your hand
   Oh I feel so. . .(*To Refrain*)

This is my four leaf clover.
I'm on the line, open mind.
This is my four leaf clover.
La la la la la la la la la la la la la la la la la (*Repeat and fade*)

JUST CHECKING

See how much you remember.

1. Listen to the recording of the steady beat and perform these patterns, patting the quarter notes and clapping the eighth notes.

2. Listen to a section of Lully's "Marche" and decide if the meter is duple or triple. Show your answer by conducting. Is the tempo slow, moderate, or fast?

3. Play the "Ode to Joy" on page 16 on keyboard, recorder, or bells as you listen to the "Historical Style Montage." Decide whether the style period of each version of the "Ode to Joy" is Renaissance, baroque, classical, romantic, or twentieth century.

4. Perform this pattern as you listen to the verse of "Run Joe" to experience the syncopated calypso style.

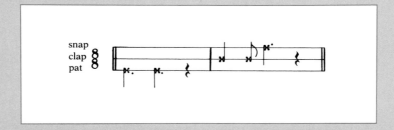

5. Use two movements to show the I and V chords as you listen to the refrain of "Run Joe." Show the chord changes by putting your palms on your desk when you hear the I chord. Put your thumbs up when you hear the V chord.

6. Listen to determine whether the style period of each of these compositions is Renaissance, baroque, classical, romantic, or twentieth century.

7. Listen to a section of Bizet's "Farandole" to determine whether its theme begins in major or minor.

8. Listen to determine whether the style of each example is African, synth-pop, Japanese, calypso, or reggae.

9. Listen to "Elements." Raise your right hand to show A sections and your left to show B sections.

10. Listen and identify the instrument family you hear in these excerpts from Lully's "Marche." Show your answer by pointing to the appropriate picture as each number is called.

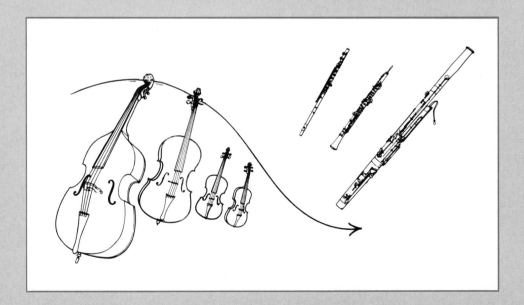

11. Listen to a section of *African Sanctus* and decide if the music sounds more African or more Western.

12. Listen to a section of *Satto* and show the dynamic changes by clapping the steady beat lightly on the palm of your hand when the music is loud. Tap the beat on the back of your hand when the music is soft.

UNIT 2

RHYTHM PLAYS A ROLE

M.C. Escher, CORDON ART, Baarn, Holland

39

DUPLE, TRIPLE, AND QUADRUPLE METER

Beats can be grouped in sets. The first beat of each group is emphasized.

- Perform this rhythm in duple meter as you listen to the recording.

"Music in Twos"

- Listen again, perform the rhythm pattern in duple meter, and play this name game. Each of you, in turn, will say your first name on the accented beat of each measure until everyone has had a turn.

- Perform this rhythm pattern in triple meter as you listen to the recording.

"Music in Threes"

- Listen again, perform the rhythm pattern, and play the name game in triple meter.

- Perform this rhythm pattern in **quadruple meter** as you listen to the recording.

"Music in Fours"

- Listen again, performing the rhythm pattern. Play a variation of the name game in which each of you says your first name on the accented first beat and your last name on the third beat.

- Show duple, triple, and quadruple meter by bouncing a tennis ball on the first beat of each measure. "Change" means to change hands.

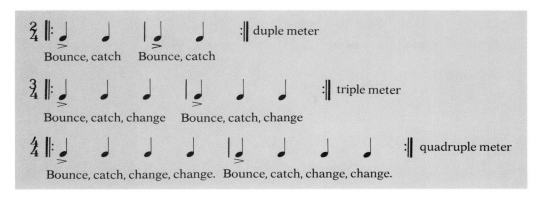

Bounce, catch   Bounce, catch   duple meter

Bounce, catch, change   Bounce, catch, change   triple meter

Bounce, catch, change, change.   Bounce, catch, change, change.   quadruple meter

- Show duple, triple, and quadruple by bouncing the ball and then by conducting as you listen to "Meter Identification Montage."

"Meter Identification Montage"

This diagram shows the conducting pattern for quadruple meter. The photograph shows how the pattern looks when the conductor faces you.

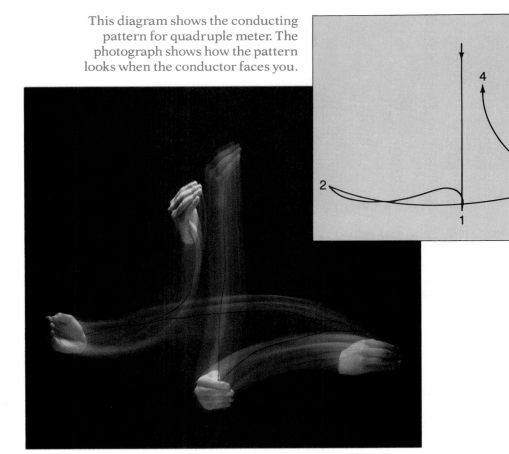

- Listen to "That's What Friends Are For." Decide when the meter changes.
- Sing the song.

That's What Friends Are For

Words and music by Carole Bayer Sager
and Burt Bacharach

And I nev - er thought I'd feel___ this way___

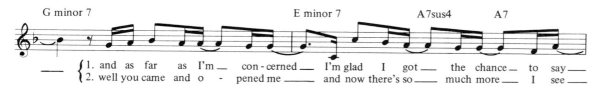

1. and as far as I'm___ con - cerned___ I'm glad I got___ the chance___ to say___
2. well you came and o - pened me _____ and now there's so _____ much more _____ I see _____

42

A STAGE STYLE

The musical *Pippin* is set in medieval times. However, because it is largely about young people growing up and learning to face the world around them, it has considerable contemporary appeal. Pippin's father, a character based on Charlemagne, wants his son to become a great warrior. Pippin, on the other hand, dreams of magic shows and miracles. Although Pippin never becomes the great warrior his father desired, he does learn to cope with the realities of being heir to the throne.

• Listen to "Love Song," which contains many changes of meter.

 "Love Song" from the musical *Pippin*, by Stephen Schwartz

A scene from the musical *Pippin*.

• Listen to "Mix 'Em Up" and raise your hand when you hear a change from one meter to another.

 "Mix 'Em Up"

- Listen again and show when the composition is in duple, triple, or quadruple meter by conducting the appropriate pattern.

 CHALLENGE As you listen to "Mix 'Em Up":

Walk forward and conduct in two when you hear duple meter. Stop and conduct in three when you hear triple meter. Stop and clap four beats in a square formation when you hear quadruple meter.

In "Love Song" Stephen Schwartz used meters of three, four, and six beats. Practice conducting the pattern for six beats in a measure.

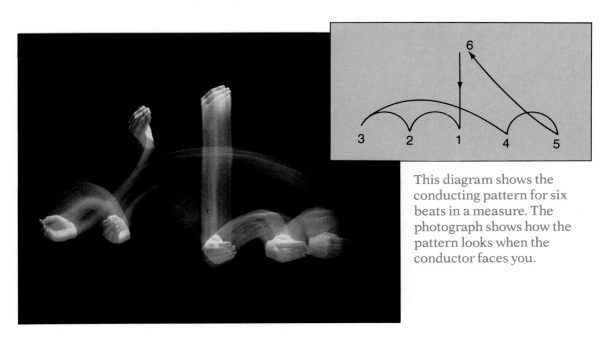

This diagram shows the conducting pattern for six beats in a measure. The photograph shows how the pattern looks when the conductor faces you.

- Look at the first four measures of "Love Song" on page 46 and decide which conducting pattern should be used in each measure.

- Practice conducting the first four measures as you listen to "Love Song."

- Sing "Love Song" (pages 46–47). Play the descant (part tinted in yellow) on recorder, bells, or keyboard.

Love Song

Words and music
by Stephen Schwartz

Sit-ting on the floor and talk-ing 'til dawn. Can-dles and con-fi-
Pri-vate lit-tle jokes and sil-ly pet names. Lav-en-der soap and
how can you de-fine a look or a touch? How can you weigh a

- den-ces. Trad-ing old be-liefs and hum-ming old songs and
lo-tions. All of the cli-chés and all of the games and
feel-ing? Ta-ken by them-selves, now they don't mean much. To-

low-er-ing old de-fen-ces. Sing-ing a   Love song,   la la la la la
all of the strange e-mo-tions. Sing-ing a
-geth-er they send you reel-ing in to a

3rd time cut to Coda ⊕

la la la la la   Love song,   la la la la la.

They say the whole is great - er____ than the sum of the parts. it's made

of. Well, if it's true of____ an - y - thing, it's true of love.

D.C. al Coda ⊕

'Cause. Love song, la la___ la la la._____

La la la la la la la la la la,

La la la la la la la la la la.

IRREGULAR METER

Much of the music you have sung and played moves in either duple, triple, or quadruple meter throughout an entire composition. Sometimes composers use changing meter in a repeating pattern to produce **irregular meter**.

This painting by the American artist Romare Bearden illustrates the spirit of jazz.

One Night Stand, Romare Bearden, CORDIER & ECKSTROM GALLERY, NY

A Little Jazz

- As you listen to the *Take Five* pattern, perform this rhythm pattern, which is a combination of triple and duple meter.

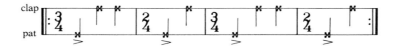

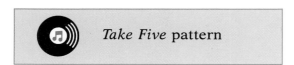

Take Five pattern

This same pattern can be written with five beats in each measure with accents on the first and fourth beats.

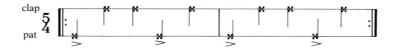

- Listen again. Show this irregular meter by patting your knees on beats 1 and 4 and clapping your hands on beats 2, 3, and 5.
- Continue patting and clapping as you play this variation on the name game. Say your first name on the first beat of your measure and your last name on the fourth beat of your measure.

Traveling in Style

- Perform the pattern in $\frac{5}{4}$ as you recite "Goin' Trav'lin'." Pat the accented beats and make a palms-up motion on each quarter rest.

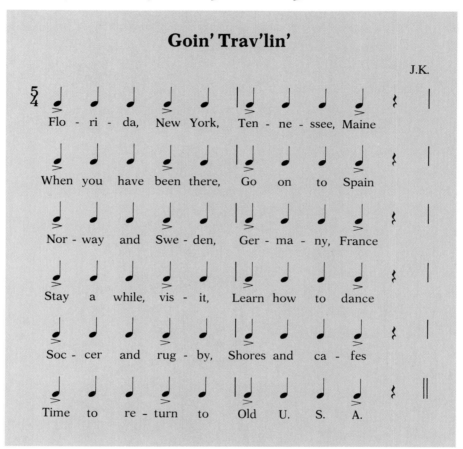

Goin' Trav'lin'

J.K.

Flo - ri - da, New York, Ten - ne - ssee, Maine

When you have been there, Go on to Spain

Nor - way and Swe - den, Ger - ma - ny, France

Stay a while, vis - it, Learn how to dance

Soc - cer and rug - by, Shores and ca - fes

Time to re - turn to Old U. S. A.

- Perform this pattern as you listen to *Take Five*. The composer, saxophonist Paul Desmond, was a member of the Dave Brubeck Quartet.

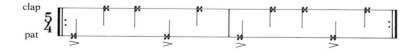

Take Five, by Paul Desmond, performed by the Dave Brubeck Quartet

Changing Meter and a Change in Style

Changing meter and irregular meter are not unique to jazz. About one hundred years before Paul Desmond wrote *Take Five*, a Russian composer was using these same techniques.

The music of Modest Mussorgsky (mo-dest′ mōō-sorg′ skē) (1839–1881) reflects his great love for his Russian homeland. He often borrowed folk melodies to use as themes for his works. Sometimes he composed original melodies that sounded like Russian folk tunes.

One of his most famous compositions is *Pictures at an Exhibition*, which he composed in memory of an artist friend, Victor Hartmann. Following Hartmann's death, a number of his paintings were exhibited in a gallery. Mussorgsky decided to compose a collection of musical "pictures" inspired by the paintings. Descriptive music of this type is called **program music**.

Mussorgsky named each section after the painting it represented, for example, "The Gnome," "The Old Castle," and "The Great Gate of Kiev." He composed a "Promenade" theme to introduce the work and to lead the listener from "picture" to "picture" as if strolling through an art gallery. This famous "Promenade" theme makes use of changing and irregular meters.

Although Mussorgsky composed *Pictures at an Exhibition* for piano alone, the French composer Maurice Ravel later arranged the work for full orchestra. It is this orchestral version with its beautiful tone colors that most people hear today.

- Listen to "Promenade" and follow the score on page 51 by pointing to the meter signature changes in each measure.

"Promenade" from Pictures at an Exhibition, by Modest Mussorgsky

- Listen again and try to determine which instruments are used to create the tone color and dynamics of each section.

Pictures at an Exhibition
Promenade

Modest Mussorgsky

A JAZZ STYLE

Unusual meters, rhythms, harmonies, forms, and tone colors have been used in jazz since 1950. You listened to *Take Five*, a composition in $\frac{5}{4}$ meter.

Unsquare Dance, composed by Brubeck, is in $\frac{7}{4}$ meter. The composer writes that this unusual meter makes *Unsquare Dance* "a challenge to the foot-tappers, finger-snappers, and hand-clappers. Deceitfully simple, it refuses to be squared."

These photographs show famous jazz musicians. Right, the Dave Brubeck Quartet; below, Gerry Mulligan; below right, Lionel Hampton (left) and Stan Getz (right).

Above, Dizzy Gillespie;
left, Thelonius Monk

Meter in Sevens

- Perform this rhythm pattern, which is a combination of duple and triple meter. Step the accented beat.

This same pattern can be written with seven beats in each measure, with the first, third, and fifth beat accented.

- Step the accented beats and make a palms-up motion on each quarter rest as you listen to *Unsquare Dance*.
- Listen to *Unsquare Dance* again and perform this **ostinato** (äs-tin-ä′ tō), or repeated pattern, on bells, recorder, or keyboard as an accompaniment.

Unsquare Dance, by Dave Brubeck

"Samiotissa" means "girl from Samos." Samos is a Greek island in the Aegean (e-jē′ ən) Sea.

54

Another Meter in Sevens

The Greek song "Samiotissa" (Girl from Samos) is in $\frac{7}{8}$ meter. This meter is similar to the meter of *Unsquare Dance*. It has seven beats to a measure. However, in "Samiotissa" different beats are accented. This shift of accent creates a completely different rhythm.

- Listen to "Samiotissa" and tap the steady beat.
- Sing "Samiotissa."

Samiotissa

English version by Stella Phredopoulos
Music by D.A. Vergoni

Sa - mio - tis - sa, Sa - mio - tis - sa, You will re-turn to Sa - mos. Sa -

- mio - tis - sa, Sa - mio - tis - sa, Is - land of beau-ty and de - light.

You will come home a-gain to me, Sa-mio-tis-sa, There's mu - sic in the sum-mer night.

You will come home a-gain to me, Sa-mio-tis-sa, There's mu - sic in the sum-mer night.

JUST CHECKING

See how much you remember.

1. Listen to the recording and decide if the meter is duple, triple, or quadruple. Show your answers by conducting.

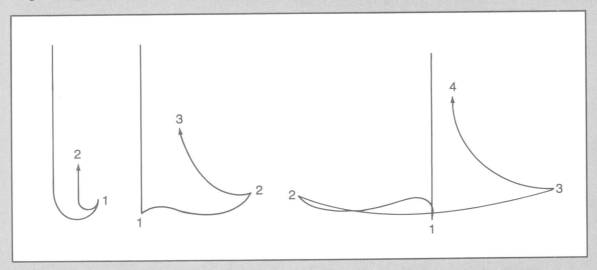

2. Listen to this musical selection, which is an example of changing meters. Identify when the meter changes by conducting the appropriate pattern. The selection begins in duple meter.

3. Perform this pattern in $\frac{5}{4}$ as you listen to "Goin' Trav'lin'" to review irregular meter.

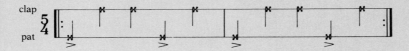

4. Perform this irregular meter pattern as you listen to *Unsquare Dance.*

5. Listen to *Take Five*. Perform a rhythm pattern that shows the meter.

6. Play part of the descant accompaniment to "Love Song" below to review changing meter. The recording has an eight-beat introduction.

7. Listen to "Love Song" and show the changes of meter by conducting the first four measures as you listen. The recording has an eight-beat introduction.

8. Clap this pattern as you listen to "Samiotissa" to review irregular meter.

9. Listen to the "Promenade" from *Pictures at an Exhibition* and show the changes of meter by clapping or patting on the first beat of each measure.

Guigass #4, Victor Vasarely,
VASARELY CENTER, NY

UNIT 3

RHYTHM SETS THE BEAT

Peacock's *Tail*, Arman, MARISA DEL RE GALLERY, NY

59

COMPOUND METER

- Clap the steady beat as you say this chant.

CHEERS

Cheers for soccer, basketball, volleyball,
Track and rugby, too.
We're for swimming, tennis, and racket ball!
Try them all—one's just right for you.

—*Jane Knox*

- As you listen to "Cheers," play the rhythm of the words on sticks or claves.

 "Cheers," by Jane Knox

In this chant the **dotted quarter note** (♩.) represents the steady beat. The basic dotted quarter-note beat can be divided into threes. The **dotted quarter rest** (𝄽·) represents one beat of silence and can also be divided into threes.

A meter that uses this steady beat might be represented as $\frac{2}{♩.}$ but is usually represented as $\frac{6}{8}$.

• Use these words to read these rhythms.

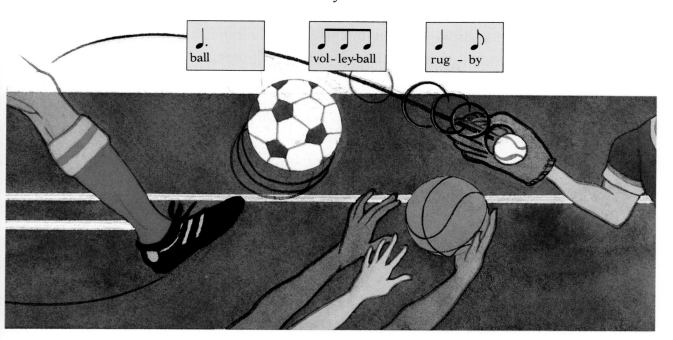

• Pat the steady dotted quarter–note beat as you say the poem.

Meter whose basic beat is subdivided into threes and/or sixes is
called **compound meter**. Some compound meters are written
as $\frac{6}{8}$, $\frac{9}{8}$, or $\frac{12}{8}$.

A SONG FROM *CATS*

Imagine a musical set in a garbage dump. Imagine a musical in which the songs are based on the poetry of a Nobel Prize winner. Imagine a musical that has no human characters, only cats. Imagine a musical in which Grizabella, an old and tattered alley cat, finds release from her sorrows and rises to heaven on a discarded automobile tire. Imagine a musical in which story, song, and dance are uniquely combined. You have imagined *Cats*, one of the most successful musicals of the past two decades.

In "Memory," Grizabella wishes her youth and beauty could return. It is probably the most familiar song from *Cats*. "Memory" contains some unusual meters and combinations of meters.

- As you listen to "Memory" notice the changes in meter.

 "Memory," from the musical *Cats*, by Andrew Lloyd Webber, Trevor Nunn, and T.S. Eliot

Left, Grizabella, who sings "Memory" in the musical *Cats*. Below, the entire cast of *Cats*. Grizabella is at the far right. This musical has been performed around the world in many languages.

When dotted quarter notes are grouped two to a measure, the meter is represented as $\frac{6}{8}$. When they are grouped four to a measure, the meter is represented as $\frac{12}{8}$.

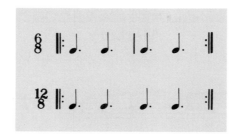

- Listen to "Memory" again and follow the score on pages 64–65. Pat the basic dotted quarter-note beat for all measures with a meter signature of $\frac{6}{8}$ or $\frac{12}{8}$.
- Listen again and divide the beat into three parts by tapping the following pattern lightly on the palm of your hand for all measures marked with a meter signature of $\frac{6}{8}$ or $\frac{12}{8}$.

- Sing the song. Look for the changing meters as you sing.

Below, a scene from *Cats*

Memory

Words by Trevor Nunn after T.S. Eliot
Music by Andrew Lloyd Webber

Mid - night.___ Not a sound from the pave - ment.___ Has the moon lost her
Mem - 'ry___ All a - lone in the moon - light___ I can smile at the

mem - 'ry?___ She is smil - ing a - lone.___ In the
old days,___ I was beau - ti - ful then.___ I re -

lamp - light the wi - thered leaves col - lect at my feet___ And the
mem - ber the time I knew what hap - pi - ness was,___ Let the

1 wind___ be - gins to moan. **2** mem - 'ry live a -

- gain. Ev - 'ry street lamp seems to beat___ a

fa - tal - is - tic warn - ing. Some - one mut - ters_ and a

poco rit.

street lamp gut - ters_ and soon it will be morn - ing.

a tempo

Day - light.___ I must wait for the sun - rise.___ I must think of a

new life___ And I must-n't give in.___ When the dawn comes to-night will be a

mem-o-ry too___ And a new day___ will be - gin.

Burnt out ends of smo - ky days.___ the

stale cold smell__ of morn - ing.___ The street lamp dies, an - o - ther

poco rit.

night is o - ver,__ an - o - ther day is dawn - ing.___

a tempo

Touch me.___ It's so ea - sy to leave me___ All a - lone with the

rall.   *a tempo*

mem - 'ry__ Of my days in the sun.___ If you touch me you'll un-der-stand what

rall.   *a tempo – slightly slower*

hap- pi -ness is. Look a new day has be - gun.

CONDUCTING IN COMPOUND METER

"Joyfully Sing" is a folk song about the joy of singing in harmony.

- Listen to Version 1 of "Joyfully Sing." Conduct in a slow six-beat pattern.

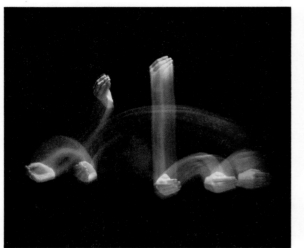

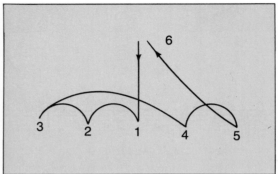

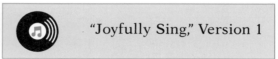

"Joyfully Sing," Version 1

- Listen to Version 2 of "Joyfully Sing," which is performed at a different tempo. Decide which conducting pattern best fits the music.

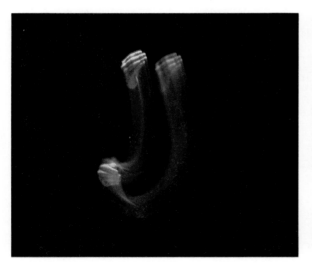

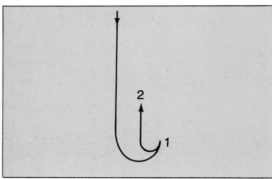

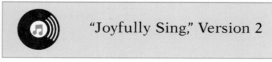

"Joyfully Sing," Version 2

When compound meter is performed at a slow tempo, it is usually conducted in the six-beat pattern. When compound meter is performed at a fast tempo, it is usually conducted in the two-beat pattern.

Joyfully Sing

Traditional German round
Arr. M.J.

Fa - la -la -la - la - la -la -la - la - la - la, joy - ful - ly, joy - ful - ly,

joy - ful - ly, fa - la -la -la - la - la - la -la - la - la - la, joy - ful - ly,

joy - ful -ly sing! Come and lift___ your voice now,

come, sing, come and sing now, lift your voice___ in

song!___ Fa - la -la -la - la - la - la -la - la - la - la, joy - ful - ly,

joy - ful - ly, joy - ful - ly, Fa - la -la -la - la - la -la - la -la - la

joy ful - ly, joy ful -ly sing! Lis -ten, lis -ten, lis -ten to our

coun - ter -point, come sing!___ We sing, in har -mo - ny sing. In

har -mo -ny sing! In har -mo -ny sing! In har -mo -ny sing!

Fields surround the village of Kaub, West Germany.

- Listen to "Joyfully Sing" (Version 2) again and identify the changes in meter.

- Perform these rhythm patterns as you listen to "Joyfully Sing" one more time.

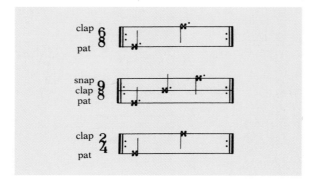

- Sing "Joyfully Sing." Look for the meter changes as you sing.

- Listen to "Compound Meter Montage" and decide which conducting pattern best fits each composition.

 "Compound Meter Montage"

CLAUDE BOLLING

Claude Bolling was born in Cannes, France, in 1930. He was a child piano prodigy and was studying harmony by the age of twelve. Bolling's interest in jazz also began at an early age. By age fifteen, he was making professional appearances throughout France as a jazz pianist. By the time he was in his mid-twenties, he had become one of the most popular jazz musicians in Europe. He has won several recording industry awards.

Bolling has also received international acclaim as an accompanist-composer. He has worked with such performers as Liza Minnelli, Jerry Lewis, Duke Ellington, and Jean-Pierre Rampal. Bolling has also written scores for dozens of French and American films.

Bolling's Suite for Violin and Jazz Piano is a unique combination of jazz and classical styles. "Caprice," a section of this suite, contains both compound and quadruple meter.

- Listen to this section of "Caprice" and raise your hand when you hear changes in meter.

 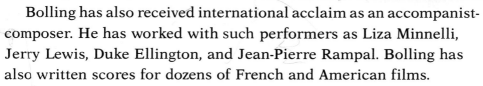

"Caprice," from Suite for Violin and Jazz Piano, by Claude Bolling

PERFORMING POLYRHYTHMS

Polyrhythm is the simultaneous combination of two or more contrasting rhythmic patterns.

"Bachi" is a musical composition that contains *polyrhythms*. The style of "Bachi" is known as *salsa*. Salsa originated in Cuba and spread quickly to the United States. It has the flavor of music from Latin America and Africa, but in addition borrows rhythms and harmonies from blues and rock.

- Listen to "Bachi" to hear polyrhythms and the sound of salsa.

 "Bachi," by Clare Fisher

You can accompany melody A of "Bachi" with several different rhythm patterns.

- Practice each new rhythm pattern in the right hand column on page 71.
- Follow the listening guide and perform each new rhythm with the recording.
- In five groups, perform all the rhythm patterns to "Bachi" to create your own polyrhythms.

Rubén Blades (center) is a popular salsa performer.

Bachi
Rhythm Accompaniment and Listening Guide

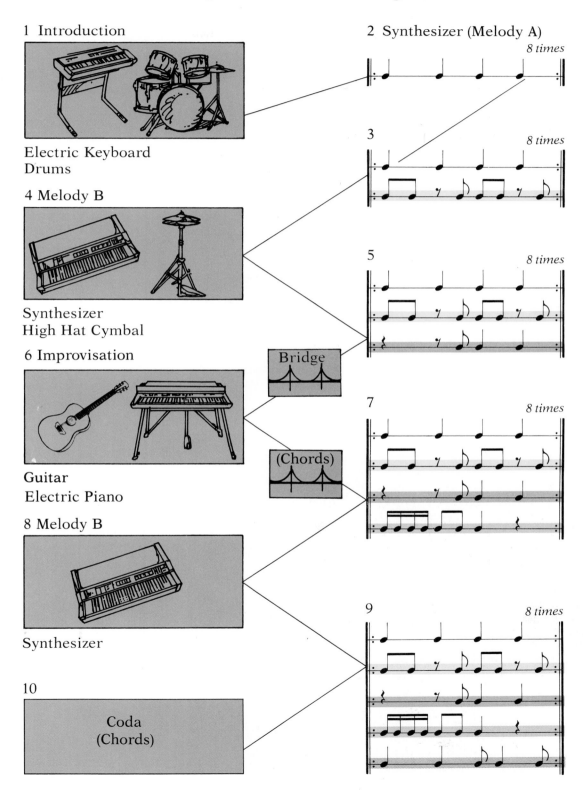

1 Introduction

Electric Keyboard
Drums

4 Melody B

Synthesizer
High Hat Cymbal

6 Improvisation

Guitar
Electric Piano

8 Melody B

Synthesizer

10

Coda
(Chords)

2 Synthesizer (Melody A)

8 times

3

8 times

5

8 times

Bridge

7

8 times

(Chords)

9

8 times

Listening to Polyrhythms

Polyrhythms are found in many different styles of music. Match the picture with the music you are hearing as you listen to "Polyrhythm Montage."

 "Polyrhythm Montage"

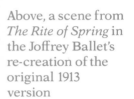

Above, a scene from *The Rite of Spring* in the Joffrey Ballet's re-creation of the original 1913 version

Above, a scene from *Cats*. The "garbage" on the stage is the same size it would appear to a real cat.

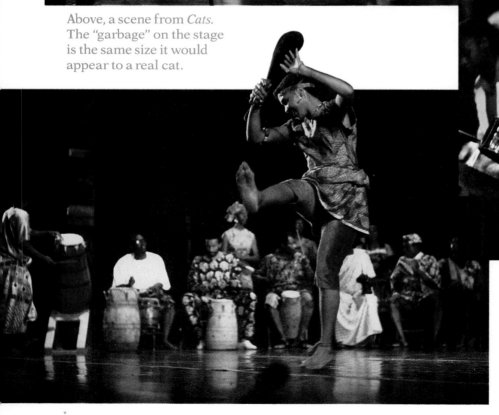

Above, a steel band from Trinidad. Left, the Ladzekpo Brothers, an African music and dance ensemble

Creating Polyrhythms

You can combine words to create different rhythm patterns.

- Read and perform each of the five rhythms in "Weather."
- Perform "Weather" to create polyrhythms.

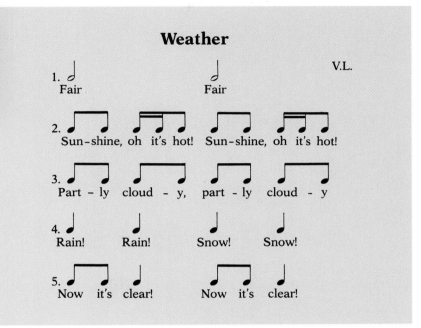

Weather

V.L.

1. Fair   Fair

2. Sun-shine, oh it's hot!   Sun-shine, oh it's hot!

3. Part – ly cloud – y,   part – ly cloud – y

4. Rain!   Rain!   Snow!   Snow!

5. Now it's clear!   Now it's clear!

- Use other words to create compositions with polyrhythms. Here are two examples.

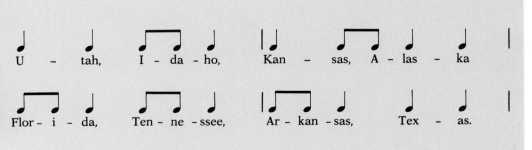

U – tah,   I – da – ho,   Kan – sas,   A – las – ka

Flor – i – da,   Ten – ne – ssee,   Ar – kan – sas,   Tex – as.

- Choose names of states, classmates, or automobiles to create your own rhythm patterns. Perform the compositions you created for your classmates. Learn and perform the polyrhythms created by your classmates. Mix and match rhythms from different compositions to create additional polyrhythms.

JUST CHECKING

See how much you remember. Listen to the recording.

1. Listen to the steady beat and perform these rhythm patterns individually and then together.

2. Listen to the steady beat and perform these rhythm patterns in
   $\frac{6}{8}$ meter by clapping as you say the words.

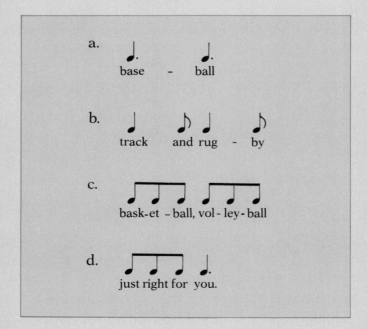

a.

base - ball

b.

track and rug - by

c.

bask-et – ball, vol - ley - ball

d.

just right for you.

74

3. Listen to these recordings and decide if the style of each example is salsa, jazz, or Broadway musical.

4. Listen to this excerpt from "Caprice" from Claude Bolling's Suite for Violin and Jazz Piano. Determine if this section is in compound or quadruple meter. Demonstrate your answer by conducting the appropriate pattern.

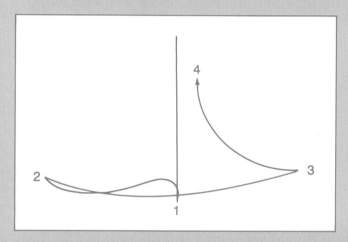 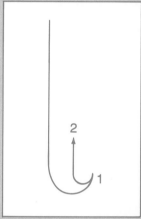

5. Listen to two contrasting selections in compound meter. In which selection does the six-beat conducting pattern fit? In which selection does the two-beat conducting pattern fit? Describe the tempo of each selection.

6. Listen to the following musical selections and decide which ones contain polyrhythms.

7. Listen to the following musical selections and decide if they are examples of simple or compound meter.

UNIT 4

MELODY

MELODY AND HARMONY

A Song in D Major

● Listen to "River" and decide how many singers and which instruments you hear.

 "River," by Bill Staines

Words and music by Bill Staines

1. I was born in the path of the win-ter wind, And was raised where the moun-tains are old.___ The spring-time___ wa-ters came danc-ing down, I re-mem-ber the tales they told.___ The whis-tling___ ways of my young-er days, Too quick-ly have fad-ed on by.___ But all of the mem-o-ries lin-ger still, Like the light in a fad-ing sky.___

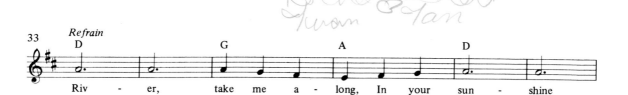

2. I've been to the city and back again;
   I've been touched by some things that I've learned,
   Met a lot of good people, and I've called them friends,
   Felt the change when the seasons turned.
   I've heard all the songs that the children sing
   And I've listened to love's melodies;
   I've felt my own music within me rise
   Like the wind in the autumn trees.

   Refrain

3. Someday when the flowers are blooming still,
   Someday when the grass is still green,
   My rolling river will round the bend
   And flow into the open sea.
   So here's to the rainbow that's followed me here,
   And here's to the friends that I know,
   And here's to the song that's within me now;
   I will sing it where'er I go.

   Refrain

The melody of "River" contains the pitches of the **D major scale.**

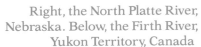

D	E	F♯	G	A	B	C♯	D	D	C♯	B	A	G	F♯	E	D
1	2	3	4	5	6	7	8	8	7	6	5	4	3	2	1

- Give the letter names of the pitches that begin and end the song.
- Which measures contain the chord symbol D?

The **home tone** D is the focus or **tone center** for "River." When music has a strong tonal center or pitch focus, it is called **tonal music.** It is said to have **tonality.**

When you play or sing two or more pitches together, you are creating **harmony.** Harmonic **consonance** results when the combination of pitches blends.

Right, the North Platte River, Nebraska. Below, the Firth River, Yukon Territory, Canada

Play this melodic accompaniment on keyboard or bells with
"River." Since it is based on the D major scale, this folklike
harmonic accompaniment is **consonant.**

Melodic Accompaniment to "River"

V.L. and M.J.

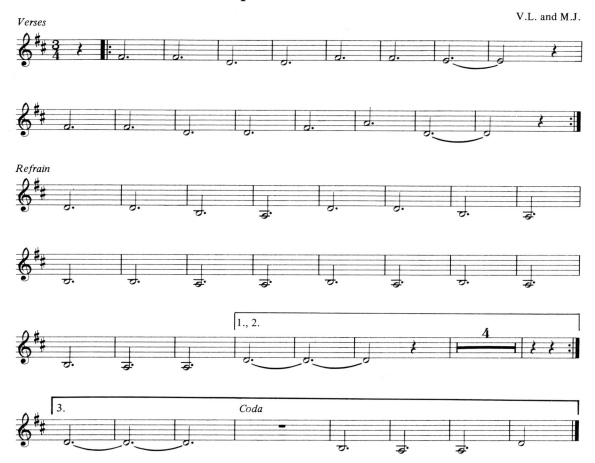

A Melody in D Major

Johann Pachelbel (yō′ hän päKH′ əl-bel) used pitches from the D
major scale in his Canon. You may have heard it in commercials
and films. The melodies follow one another and, when combined,
create harmony.

- Listen to the Canon to hear how Pachelbel used a major scale as
  a basis for the melodies.

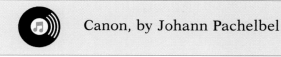

Canon, by Johann Pachelbel

TEXTURE IN MUSIC

Performing a Canon

A **canon** is a musical composition in two or more voice parts.
A musical phrase is started by one voice and repeated exactly by
successive voices, which begin before the first voice has ended. The
combination of voices produces harmony.

"Ahrirang" is a Korean folk song about the Ahrirang Pass in the
mountains near the city of Seoul.

• Learn to sing "Ahrirang" as a canon.

Ahrirang

Korean folk song
English words by M.S.

Ⓐ *Refrain*
Ah - ri - rang, Ah - ri - rang, Ah - ra - ri - yo,____

Walk - ing o - ver roll - ing hills__ of__ Ah - ri - rang.
Time goes ver - y slow - ly far a - way from Ah - ri - rang.

Ⓑ *Verses*
Walk - ing slow - ly to some place__ far,__ far a - way
Back a - gain o - ver tall hills__ of__ Ah - ri - rang

Hop - ing to re - turn a - gain to Ah - ri - rang____ some day.
Once a - gain re - turn - ing home__ to__ Ah - ri - rang.

>
> **CHALLENGE** Try to perform "Ahrirang" as a canon by clapping the rhythm of
> the melody without singing it.

Musical Texture

Texture in music refers to the way layers of sound are combined. When you sang "Ahrirang" the first time without accompaniment, you sang in unison. Unison singing creates a texture known as **monophonic**, meaning one sound.

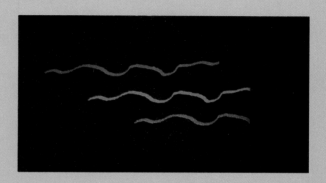

When you sang "Ahrirang" as a canon, you created a texture know as **polyphonic** (po-lē-fo'nik), meaning many voices sounding together.

When you sang "River," the melody was in the foreground with accompaniment in the background. This texture is called **homophonic**.

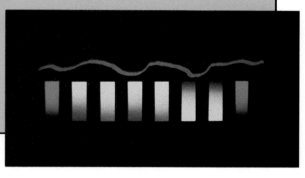

An **oratorio** is a large musical work for solo voices, chorus, and orchestra performed without special costumes or scenery. The "Hallelujah" Chorus from George Frederick Handel's oratorio *Messiah* is one of the most famous choral works in the English language. Handel creates harmonic interest by setting the text in monophonic, polyphonic, and homophonic textures.

The word *hallelujah* is stated and restated by different sections of the chorus almost like a cheering section. Other lines of the text are sung solemnly to emphasize their serious message, and for contrast. The festive quality of the piece is made even more brilliant by the trumpets and timpani. The story is told that at one of the first performances, the English king, George II, was so moved by the music that he stood up to show his approval.

• Identify the texture you hear when a number is called. The four
  main themes are shown.

 "Hallelujah" Chorus from *Messiah*, by George Frederick Handel

Versailles (vair-sǐ′) Cathedral, France, is in the baroque style.

1. Introduction

2. Theme A

Hal - le - lu - jah, Hal - le - lu - jah, Hal - le - lu - jah, Hal - le - lu - jah, Hal -

- le - lu - jah,

3. Theme B

for the Lord God Om - nip - o - tent reign - eth. Hal - le -

- lu - jah, Hal - le - lu - jah, Hal - le - lu - jah, Hal - le - lu - jah,

4. Theme B repeated higher

for the Lord God Om - nip - po - tent reign - eth. Hal - le -

lu - jah! Hal - le - lu - jah! Hal - le - lu - jah! Hal - le - lu - jah!

5. Theme C

The king - dom of this world is be - come

6. Theme D

And He shall reign for ev – er and ev – er

7. "King of Kings and Lord of Lords" is heard in long note values;
   "forever and ever" is added in shorter note values. Gradually,
   this moves higher and higher.

8. Theme D repeated

And He shall reign for ev – er and ev – er,

9. "King of Kings and Lord of Lords" is heard in long note values;
   "forever and ever" is added in shorter note values.

10. The coda ends with four "hallelujahs" followed by a dramatic
    pause and a final "hallelujah" in very long note values.

George Frederick Handel, Thomas Hudson. By courtesy of the
NATIONAL PORTRAIT GALLERY, London

GEORGE FREDERICK HANDEL

George Frederick Handel (1685–1759) is one of the two most respected and revered musicians of the baroque period. He and Johann Sebastian Bach created musical compositions that brought the baroque period to its peak.

Handel was born in Germany in 1685, and began his formal musical training at the age of eight. In his early twenties he visited Italy and was impressed and influenced by the Italian baroque musical style. After leaving Italy, he went to England and became a favorite of the royal family. He became a British citizen in 1726.

Handel is remembered today for the English oratorios he wrote later in his life. However, he was probably more well known in his day for the fine Italian-style operas he wrote and produced. His most famous oratorio, *Messiah*, was composed in 1741 in less than three weeks and was an immediate success. On April 6, 1759, when completely blind, Handel conducted a performance of *Messiah* in London. Eight days later he died and was buried in Westminster Abbey.

A NEW WAY TO ORGANIZE A MELODY

Composers use different techniques to create and develop melodies.

- Read "Backward Bill." What repeated word in the poem suggests how a composer might work with a melody?

Backward Bill

Backward Bill, Backward Bill,
He lives way up on Backward Hill,
Which is really a hole in the sandy ground
(But that's a hill turned upside down).

Backward Bill's got a backward shack
With a big front porch that's built out back.
You walk through the window and look out the door
And the cellar is up on the very top floor.

Backward Bill he rides like the wind
Don't know where he's going but sees where he's been.
His spurs they go "neigh" and his horse it goes "clang."
And his six-gun goes "gnab," it never goes "bang."

Backward Bill's got a backward pup,
They eat their supper when the sun comes up,
And he's got a wife named Backward Lil,
"She's my own true hate," says Backward Bill.

Backward Bill wears his hat on his toes
And puts on his underwear over his clothes.
And come every payday he pays his boss,
And rides off a-smilin' a-carryin' his hoss.

—*Shel Silverstein*

Day and Night is by the Dutch artist M. C. Escher. Each side of this woodcut is the reverse of the other.

- Perform "Retrograde in D Major" on keyboard, recorder, or bells. The melody in measures 9–16 is a backward version of measures 1–8. The last tone in measure 8 becomes the first tone in measure 9. When a melodic pattern is reversed so that its beginning becomes its end, it is called a *retrograde*.

Retrograde in D major

- Compare the pitches of the melody in measures 1–8 with measures 9–16. Are the phrases of equal length? Are the same pitches used in both sections?

- Perform "Rhythms in Retrograde."

Rhythms in Retrograde

V.L. and M.J.

- Choose percussion instruments and perform "Rhythms in Retrograde."
- Perform "Sounds in Retrograde."

Sounds in Retrograde

V.L.

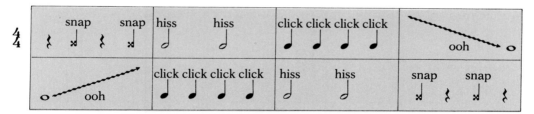

- Perform "Rhythms in Retrograde" and "Sounds in Retrograde" in combination.

 CHALLENGE Create, notate, and perform your own retrograde sound piece.

A NEW KIND OF PITCH ORGANIZATION

Twelve-Tone Music

- Count all the black and white keys to determine the number of different pitches from C to B on the keyboard.

One kind of twentieth-century music is **twelve-tone,** or **serial,** music. In this musical style, the composer organizes all twelve tones in a **row.**

The song "The Web" is based on a twelve-tone row. It also makes use of retrograde. Here is the original tone row upon which "The Web" is based.

- Play this tone row on bells or keyboard.

- Play the retrograde on bells or keyboard.

- Follow the score as you listen to "The Web." Identify the words where the retrograde begins.

The Web

Words by Susan Lucas
Music by David Ward-Steinman

- Sing "The Web" or play it on bells or keyboard with the instrumental parts.

In twelve-tone music, all twelve tones are played in the order the composer has chosen until each tone has been used once. The row is deliberately organized so that the melody has no tonal center. When a melody has no tonal center or tonic pitch to which all other tones relate, it is called **atonal.**

- The composer of "The Web" decided to use a tone row to organize the pitches of this song. He also chose to use retrograde. Suggest a reason why he might have done it.
- Create your own atonal composition by:

  1. Choosing an order in which to play each of the twelve tones without repetition of any tone to create an atonal melody
  2. Deciding on a meter and a rhythmic pattern for your melody
  3. Reversing the order of the melody, playing it backward, in retrograde

---

 CHALLENGE Add an instrumental steady beat, a rhythmic ostinato, or a body percussion accompaniment to your melody. Find a way to notate your composition.

Wassily Kandinsky painted *Improvisation XIV* in 1910, about ten years before Arnold Schoenberg introduced twelve-tone music.

Expressionism in Music

Arnold Schoenberg (shən′ berg) (1874–1951) is known as one of the leaders of *expressionism* in music. The **expressionist** movement became popular in the early twentieth century. It was a movement in which artists—painters, composers, or authors—tried to produce works that expressed their own feelings about an object or event, rather than depicting the object itself in a realistic manner.

In music this type of creative activity required some new method of dealing with notes, chords, tone colors, and rhythms. Schoenberg first introduced twelve-tone, or serial, music around 1920. His new approach to composing often shocked people. He took away things they expected to hear. Melodies did not always sound "pretty." There were no major or minor harmonies.

• Listen to this example of Schoenberg's work.

 Begleitungsmusik zu einer Lichtspielscene (excerpt), Op. 34, by Arnold Schoenberg

Expressionist styles developed in art as well as in music. The painting on the right is a portrait of Arnold Schoenberg, done in 1917. Below, an expressionist painting by the Norwegian artist Edvard Munch.

Girls on the Bridge. Edvard Munch, NATIONAL GALLERY, Oslo

Portrait of Arnold Schoenberg, Egon Schiele

JUST CHECKING

See how much you remember. Listen to the recording.

1. Listen to the recording and perform these melodies by singing or playing the bells or keyboard. The recording has a four-measure introduction.

a.

b.

2. The harmony you just performed could best be described as:
   atonal and dissonant   tonal and consonant

3. Perform or listen to "Ahrirang" as a canon.

4. Listen to the last part of "River" and identify the home tone by humming it or playing it on keyboard, recorder, or bells.

5. Listen to a portion of the "Hallelujah" Chorus and determine whether the texture is monophonic, polyphonic, or homophonic. Show your answer by pointing to the diagram that shows the texture as each number is called.

monophonic   polyphonic   homophonic

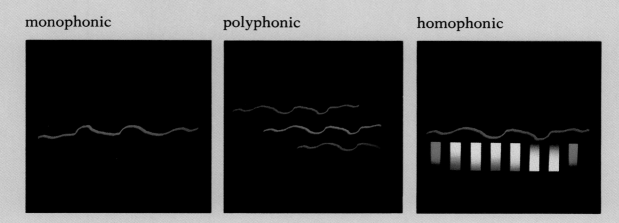

6. Perform the following body percussion to review *retrograde*.

Rhythms in Retrograde

V.L. and M.J.

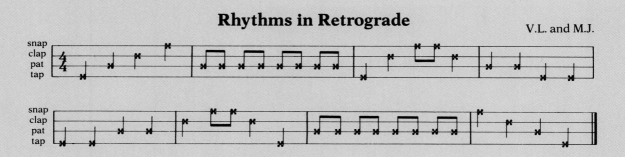

7. Listen to "The Web" to review melodic retrograde. In which measures is the melodic pattern reversed so that its end becomes its beginning?

8. On keyboard or bells play the following pitches that make up the twelve-tone row on which the melody of "The Web" is based.

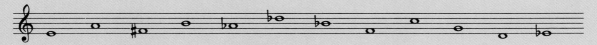

9. Play the retrograde of this tone row on keyboard or bells.

UNIT 5

HARMONY

CHANGING KEYS

Pictures Through Music

The music of the gospel song "Climbing Up to Zion" reflects the meaning of the words.

● Follow the different ways the melody is presented as you listen to the song. Decide whether the melody sounds higher or lower each time it repeats.

 "Climbing Up to Zion," by Wintley Phipps

● Sing the melody.

Climbing Up to Zion

Words and music by Wintley Phipps

WINTLEY PHIPPS

Wintley Phipps has traveled an unusual path to his career in religious music. He was born in Trinidad, West Indies, but raised in Montréal, Canada. Although familiar with hymns and church music from his early childhood, he did not come into contact with African American gospel music until his college days in Alabama. It was there that he started composing.

After earning a master's degree in divinity, Reverend Phipps knew that he would be devoting his life to church work. His love of music, however, continued. Today, Reverend Phipps both composes and performs his unique multicultural music.

Gospel Music

Gospel music is a type of religious music that originated in the South. It developed in African American Baptist churches during the 1930s, and quickly became more widely known. By the 1940s and 1950s radio stations all over the country played songs by such gospel singers as Rosetta Tharpe and Mahalia Jackson.

Gospel is different from other forms of African American religious music. The composer is usually known. The songs have instrumental accompaniments, and the melodies are complex with nontraditional harmonies. Gospel music, like jazz, has many polyrhythms. Early lyrics were based on the gospels but later became expressions of personal experience.

Gospel music has influenced rhythm and blues and soul music. The foot-stomping frenzy of gospel blended naturally into the intensely expressive soul music of James Brown, Otis Redding, and Ray Charles. A great number of rhythm and blues singers got their start by singing gospel music in church, including Aretha Franklin and Dionne Warwick.

Changing the Key for Effect

"Mi Caballo Blanco" is a popular song by Francisco Flores del Campo (frän-sēs′ kō flō′ res del käm′ pō) that describes the devotion of the South American ranchers for their horses. As in "Climbing Up to Zion," the composer moves the melody into different scales, or **keys**, to create an effect.

• Listen and decide if the song moves to higher or lower keys.

 "Mi Caballo Blanco," by Francisco Flores del Campo

Mi Caballo Blanco

Words and music by
Francisco Flores del Campo

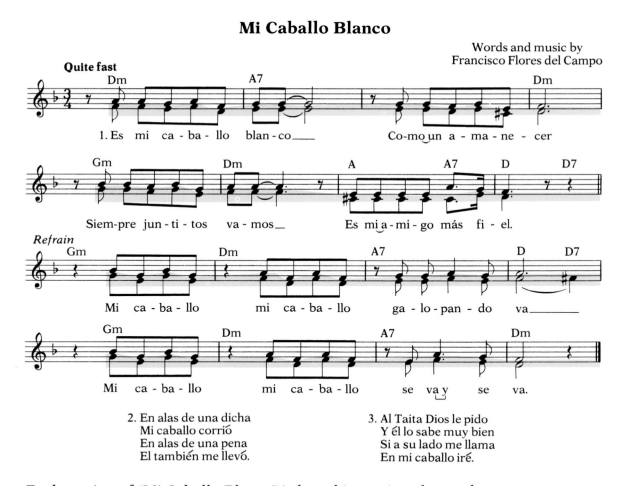

2. En alas de una dicha
   Mi caballo corrió
   En alas de una pena
   El también me llevó.

3. Al Taita Dios le pido
   Y él lo sabe muy bien
   Si a su lado me llama
   En mi caballo iré.

Each section of "Mi Caballo Blanco" is based in a minor key and starts on a different pitch. The change from a section of music based on one scale to a section of music based on another scale is called **modulation**.

100

- Perform these three melodic accompaniments to "Mi Caballo Blanco." They are based on the D minor, E minor, and F minor scales.

Melodic Accompaniment to "Mi Caballo Blanco"

- Sing the song and perform the accompaniments.

Creating Variety in Music

Composers use modulation to create interest and variety in their compositions.

- Follow the chart as you listen to the opening section of Concertino for Flute and Orchestra by Cécile Chaminade (se-sēl′ sha-mē-näd′). The theme is stated several times.

 Concertino for Flute and Orchestra, by Cécile Chaminade

1. Statement of theme (key of D major)

2. Statement of theme (key of A major)

3. Statement of theme (key of B♭ major)

4. Statement of theme (key of D major)

- Listen again and decide how the composer uses dynamics and **register,** the high to low range of a voice or instrument, to create interest and variety.

102

CÉCILE CHAMINADE

Cécile Chaminade (1857–1944) made her first appearance as a concert pianist at the age of eighteen in her native Paris. She was an illustrious piano soloist and conductor, and traveled widely in France, England, and the United States from 1892 until well into the twentieth century. An active composer as well as performer, Cécile Chaminade is remembered mainly for her elegant piano compositions, many of which she performed in concert.

THE BLUES—AN AMERICAN STYLE

Playing the Twelve-Bar Blues

The **blues** is a style of music that was created by African Americans around the turn of the century. The words to blues songs are usually about loneliness, sadness, or lost love. The blues has its own scale and chord pattern called the **twelve-bar blues.**

- Listen to early blues singer Gertrude "Ma" Rainey sing "Hear Me Talking to You." Identify the instruments that accompany the performance.

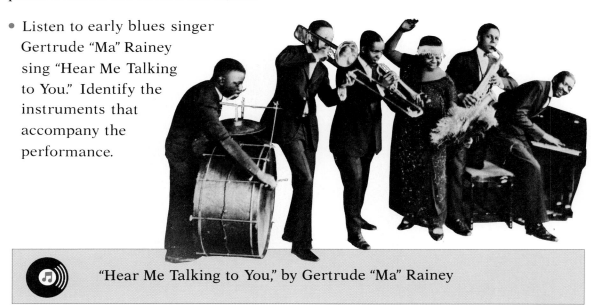

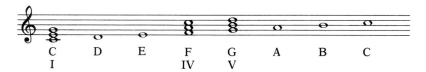
"Hear Me Talking to You," by Gertrude "Ma" Rainey

Blues harmony is based on three chords of the major scale: the tonic (I) chord, the dominant (V) chord, and the chord based on the fourth pitch of the scale called the **subdominant** or **IV chord.** You can play an accompaniment for all traditional blues songs once you learn these three chords.

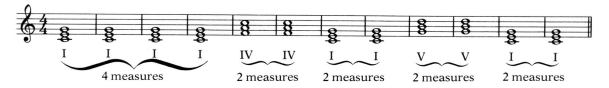

This twelve-bar accompaniment to "Hear Me Talking to You" shows a twelve-bar blues pattern.

104

- Learn to play the chords in the twelve-bar blues. Then play them with the song.
- Create your own melody and words to go with the twelve-bar blues.

WILLIAM GRANT STILL

William Grant Still (1895–1978) is often referred to as the dean of African American composers. Best known for his music using African American and other American folk songs, he received many awards and honors as the result of his outstanding work.

Still grew up in a middle-class family in Mississippi and Arkansas and was exposed to various styles of popular and classical music, including both opera and blues. From a very early age he heard his grandmother sing hymns, gospel songs, and spirituals. His father, a band leader and cornet player, died while Still was quite young. Later, his stepfather encouraged his musical development by sharing his collection of opera records, taking him to concerts, and providing him with private music lessons.

Still arranged and composed music and directed the band at his college. In 1916 he studied with the French composer Edgar Varèse, further developing his composing skills.

The 1931 premiere of Still's *Afro-American Symphony* by the Rochester Symphony under Howard Hanson was the first performance by a major symphony orchestra of a symphonic work by an African American composer. Later, Still became the first African American to conduct a major American orchestra, the Los Angeles Philharmonic. In 1949 his opera *Troubled Island* was the first composed by an African American to be performed by a major opera company, the New York City Opera. He was also one of the first African American composers to write music for radio, films, and television.

The Blues in a Symphony

Theme A of the first movement of William Grant Still's *Afro-American Symphony* is based on the twelve-bar blues. The overall mood of the music is one of longing, and is related to this verse of Paul Laurence Dunbar that was later applied to the music.

> All my life long twell de night has pas'
> Let de wo'k come es it will,
> So dat I fin' you, my honey, at last,
> Somewaih des ovah de hill.

- Follow the map as you listen to the first movement of *Afro-American Symphony*. The term **pizzicato** (pit-zi-kä′ tō) in boxes 2 and 9 tells the string players to pluck the strings instead of using the bow.

 Afro-American Symphony, First Movement, by William Grant Still

INTRODUCTION

1 THEME A

SOLO

2 THEME A

SOLO

PIZZICATO

3

FULL ORCHESTRA

AND FASTER

THEN

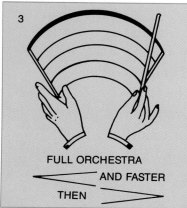

4 THEME B

SOLO   WITH OTHER STRINGS

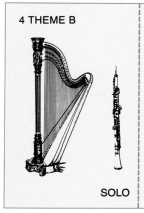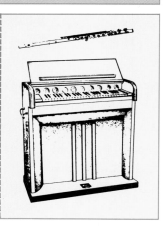

5 THEME B

WITH OTHER STRINGS

6 THEME B (IN MINOR)

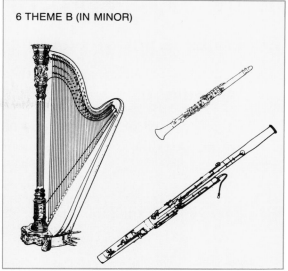

7 THEME A TRANSFORMED

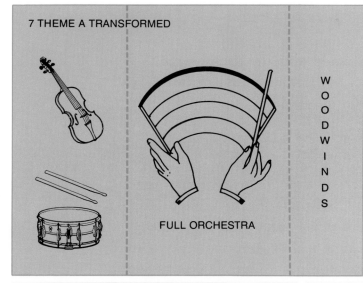

FULL ORCHESTRA

WOODWINDS

8 THEME B (IN MINOR)

9 THEME A

PIZZICATO

WITH WOODWINDS

10 CODA

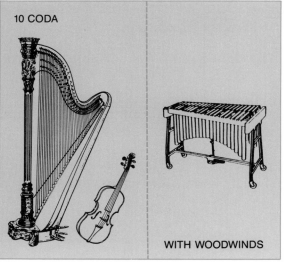

WITH WOODWINDS

107

TYPES OF HARMONY

Consonance and Dissonance

Tones that do not seem to sound as though they go together are called **dissonant**.

- Play the first part of "America" on bells or keyboard with this recording. Does the music sound consonant or dissonant? Why?

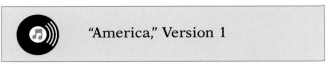

"America," Version 1

- Play the first part of "America" again with the recording of Version 2. Does the music sound consonant or dissonant? Why?

"America," Version 2

The dissonance in harmony in Version 2 of "America" was created by using two different tonal centers or scales at the same time. When music has two tonal centers at the same time, it is called **bitonal**. The bitonal harmony in Version 2 of "America" was written by the twentieth-century American composer Charles Ives as part of a set of variations on the song "America." The variations were written for pipe organ.

The right hand plays harmony based on the F major scale.

The left hand plays harmony based on the D♭ major scale.

108

- Listen to *Variations on "America"* to determine how the composer used different types of harmony, dynamics, and rhythm to create interest and variety.

 Variations on "America," by Charles Ives

1. Introduction: Based on the beginning of the song; phrase "My country, 'tis of thee" most prominent; *ff*

2. "America": Presented in a traditional style; harmony consonant; *pp*

3. First Variation: Melody in bass with continually moving sixteenth notes above melody; *pp*

4. Second Variation: New harmonization of the theme much like the close harmony of a barbershop quartet

5. Interlude: Theme played as a canon; in bitonal harmony

6. Third Variation: Change of rhythm, which produces an effect similar to a calliope; *f*

7. Fourth Variation: Rhythm for theme based in the style of a polonaise, a dance of Poland; now based on a minor scale

8. Interlude: Again uses dissonant bitonal harmony

9. Fifth Variation: Melody played on the keyboard; contrasting line in the pedal part (the lowest part); directions to organists say to play the pedal part as fast as the feet can go

10. Coda: Described by Ives as "in a way a kind of take-off on the Bunker Hill fight."

This work is typical of Ives's strongly original style of music. He takes a recognized melody and treats it in a very creative way.

 CHALLENGE Create your own variations on "America." Change the rhythm, the tempo, or the style.

CHARLES IVES

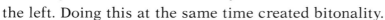

Charles Ives (1874–1954) grew up in a small town in Connecticut where his father was the local bandmaster. He received his early musical training from his father, who encouraged him to experiment with all sorts of sound combinations to "stretch his ears." Ives liked the harsh dissonance created by playing "America" in one key with the right hand at the keyboard and in another key with the left. Doing this at the same time created bitonality.

As a teenager Ives became a church organist, and one can imagine that he enjoyed shocking the congregation by changing the harmonies of familiar songs like "America."

Because he thought his unconventional music was not going to be popular, Ives went into the insurance business. Eventually he founded a successful insurance agency and became very wealthy. However, music remained his first love, and he continued to compose evenings and weekends.

Ives found ideas for his music in the folk and popular music he knew as a boy: hymns, ragtime, village band concerts, church choir music, patriotic songs, and dances. Perhaps it was these sounds that gave him the idea for his *Variations on "America,"* written for pipe organ.

110

TELLING A STORY
THROUGH MELODY AND HARMONY

Franz Schubert's "The Erlking" is one of the finest examples of *art song* romanticism. An **art song** is a composition for solo voice and instrumental accompaniment, usually keyboard. The term *art song* is used to distinguish such songs from folk songs and popular songs. In the text to "The Erlking" the German poet Johann Wolfgang von Goethe (gə(r)′ tə) tells of a father riding on horseback through a storm with his child in his arms. The boy, who is very sick with a high fever, remembers the legend that whoever is touched by the king of the elves, the Erlking, must die.

"The Erlking" has four separate characters. Usually all are sung by one person. Schubert uses a wide range of pitches and contrasts in vocal registers to depict each of the four characters. Contrasts of major and minor tonality also help to identify the characters.

- Listen to the beginning of "The Erlking," and choose one word to describe the mood. Which of these musical characteristics do you think help to express that mood?

    major/minor   soft/loud   fast/slow

 "The Erlking," by Franz Schubert

- Listen to "The Erlking" and follow the translation of the German text.

111

The Erlking

Narrator

1. Who is that riding like the wind through the night?
   It is a father, holding his child.
   He holds him safely in his arms,
   He holds him tightly and keeps him warm.

Father

2. "My son, why do you hide your face so anxiously?"

Son

3. "Father, don't you see the Erlking?
   The Erlking with his crown and his train?"

Father

4. "My son, it is a streak of mist."

Erlking

5. "Ah, small boy, come away with me.
   We'll play the greatest games with you.
   We'll walk by the river, see beautiful flowers.
   My mother has fantastic clothes for you."

Son

6. "My father, my father, don't you hear
   the Erlking whispering promises to me?"

Father

7. "Be quiet, stay quiet, my child;
   the wind is rustling in the dead leaves."

Erlking

8. "Ah, fine boy, are you sure you won't come with me?
My daughters will take good care of you.
There'll be parties every night—singing, dancing.
They'll cradle and dance you, and sing you a lullaby."

Son

9. "My father, my father, and don't you see there
the Erlking's daughters in the shadows?"

Father

10. "My son, my son, I see it clearly;
the old willows look so gray."

Erlking

11. "I must have you with me.
If you won't come, then I will use force!"

Son

12. "My father, my father, now he is taking hold of me!
The Erlking has hurt me!"

Narrator

13. The father shudders, he rides swiftly on,
he holds in his arms the groaning child,
he reaches the courtyard weary and anxious;
in his arms the child was dead.

● Listen again to "The Erlking," and answer these questions.

How do dynamics create the mood?
How does the piano accompaniment set the mood of the story?
Which character sings in major?
Why is the remainder of the song in minor?

 "The Erlking," by Franz Schubert

 CHALLENGE Think of your favorite songs. Which song seems to use dynamics, accompaniment, and major or minor most effectively to set a mood? Compare this to how Schubert set the mood in "The Erlking." Share your song with your classmates.

Schubert Playing the Piano, Gustav Klimt

Schubert Playing the Piano is by the Austrian artist Gustav Klimt (1872–1918). Klimt chose to paint the scene in a romantic style.

A view of Vienna in Schubert's time

FRANZ SCHUBERT

Franz Schubert, drawing after a water-color by W.A. Rieder

The music of every important composer has something special to offer. In the case of Franz Schubert (1797–1828), it is outstanding melodies, easily remembered for their beauty and simplicity.

Growing up in Austria as the son of a schoolmaster, Schubert received his musical training as a choirboy in the Royal Chapel. Schubert also began a teaching career, but soon abandoned this to devote himself entirely to music.

Schubert composed over six hundred songs for voice and piano, and once composed eight songs in one day. Besides songs, he composed instrumental music including symphonies, chamber music, and solo piano music. Schubert's world-famous "Unfinished" Symphony (so called because it has only two movements instead of the usual four) contains many beautiful melodies. Occasionally Schubert used melodies from his own songs as themes for his instrumental pieces as in the "Trout" Quintet for Piano and Strings and the String Quartet No. 14 in D Minor, known as the "Death and the Maiden" Quartet. Schubert's music also is important in that his style bridges the classical and romantic periods.

115

JUST CHECKING

See how much you remember.

1. Perform this melodic pattern on recorder, bells, or keyboard.

2. Perform this twelve bar blues harmonic progression on bells or keyboard.

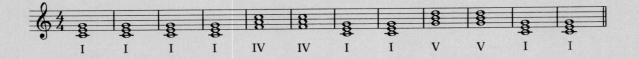

3. Listen to part of "Climbing Up to Zion" to review modulation. Decide if the melody sounds higher or lower each time it repeats.

4. Listen to a section of the Concertino for Flute and Orchestra and decide how the composer uses dynamics and register to create interest and variety.

5. Listen and determine whether the style period for each of these examples is romantic, twentieth century, blues, or gospel.

6. Listen and determine whether the harmony in each example sounds more consonant or dissonant.

7. Listen to a section of "Mi Caballo Blanco" and raise your hand when you hear the music modulate.

8. Listen to a section of "Mi Caballo Blanco" and decide if the music modulates to a higher or lower key.

9. As you listen to these examples from "The Erlking," decide which character is singing, based on whether you hear major or minor and the register of the melody.

10. Listen to Theme A of the *Afro-American Symphony*. Identify the instrumental tone color by naming the picture that best describes what you are hearing.

INTRODUCTION

1 THEME A

SOLO

2 THEME A

SOLO

PIZZICATO

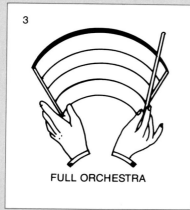

3

FULL ORCHESTRA

4 THEME B

SOLO

WITH OTHER STRINGS

Dolmen in the Snow, Johann Christian Clausen Dahl,
MUSEUM DER BILDENDEN KÜNSTE, Leipzig

UNIT **6**

FORM
AND
STYLE

Three Flags (1958), Jasper Johns, WHITNEY MUSEUM OF AMERICAN ART, NY

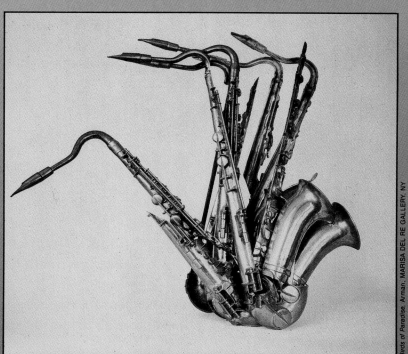

Birds of Paradise, Arman, MARISA DEL RE GALLERY, NY

119

BUILDING BLOCKS OF FORM

Phrases can be described as the building blocks of form. A **phrase** is a complete musical idea. Phrases of equal length contain the same number of beats or measures.

As you listen to "Two-Chord Strut":

- Clap the beat to show the length of the first phrase.
- Snap the beat to show the length of the next phrase.
- Move your hands in an arc to show the length of the phrases.

clap   snap

 "Two-Chord Strut,"
by Michael Treni

As you listen to "Two-Chord Strut" again:

- Step the beat to show the length of the first phrase.
- Stand still and move your hands in an arc to show the length of the next phrase.
- Listen to "Three-Chord Strut," and change your movement patterns as you step each phrase.

"Three-Chord Strut,"
by Michael Treni

In "Two-Chord Strut" and "Three-Chord Strut" most of the phrases are the same length. In the song "Careless Whisper," the composers George Michael and Andrew Ridgeley use layers of phrases of different lengths to create interest and variety.

- Play this melodic accompaniment to "Careless Whisper" on keyboard, bells, or guitar as you listen to the song.

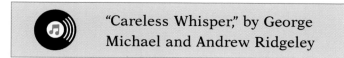
- Listen again and play this chord pattern on keyboard, bells, or guitar to accompany the song.

This four-measure chord pattern repeats throughout the song. It establishes a **harmonic phrase** that is sixteen beats long.

- Listen to the opening section of "Careless Whisper." Focus on the number of beats in the phrases performed by the saxophone and the singer.

"Careless Whisper" has phrases that are four beats, eight beats, and sixteen beats long. The phrases played on the saxophone are four beats in length. The phrases sung by the lead singer are generally eight beats in length. The harmonic phrase is sixteen beats in length, formed by the four-measure chord patterns.

- As you listen to "Careless Whisper" again, show the three different phrase lengths by moving your hand in an arc from left to right.

Wham!

George Michael and Andrew Ridgeley of the British group Wham! first met in school in their hometown of Bushey, England. George and Andrew wanted to be pop stars, and in their first group, the Executives, they started writing songs together. Although they were making records as Wham! as early as 1980, they did not produce a top American hit until the release of "Wake Me Up Before You Go-Go" in 1984. Other Wham! hits were "Freedom," "I'm Your Man," and "Christmas."

Wham! achieved international status after the release of "Careless Whisper" in 1985. At the invitation of the Youth Federation of China, Wham! became the first major Western rock band to perform in the People's Republic. Following the release of their third album *Music From the Edge of Heaven*, in 1986, George and Andrew broke up as a duo to follow solo careers.

Wham! in performance.

George Michael and Andrew Ridgeley

PHRASES OF DIFFERENT LENGTHS

In "Careless Whisper" the composers used layers of phrases
containing four, eight, and sixteen beats. Each layer was made
up of phrases with the same number of beats. In "(Life Is a)
Celebration," Rick Springfield uses another technique with phrases
to create interest and variety.

- As you listen to "(Life Is a) Celebration," decide if the phrases are
  all the same length.

 "(Life Is a) Celebration" by Rick Springfield

- Listen again and move your hand in an arc on each phrase.
- Sing the song.

"(Life Is a) Celebration"

Words and music by
Rick Springfield

Life is a cel-e-bra-tion, come on now and cel-e-brate, cel-e-brate.

Life is a cel-e-bra-tion, look it's a rev-e-la-tion, so

cel-e-brate now, cel-e - brate life. Cel-e-brate now, cel-e - brate life.

cel-e-brate now, cel-e - brate life. Cel-e-brate now, cel-e - brate life.

Cel - e-brate now, cel-e - brate life.

Cel - e-brate now, cel-e - brate life.

How could I have been so blind, just to think that we were

You came a - long and I was no

liv - ing to die?

lon - ger a - lone, and you led me to the light.

And you showed me Life is a cel-e-bra - tion, and

Lord, I'm gon-na cel - e-brate. Life is a cel-e-bra - tion,

I

Life is a cel-e-bra - tion,

II cresc.

come on now_ and cel-e-brate, cel-e-brate.

ff

look it's a rev-e-la - tion. So cel-e-brate now, cel-e - brate life.

Cel-e-brate now, cel-e - brate life.

To Coda ⊕

Cel-e-brate now, cel-e - brate life. Cel-e-brate now, cel-e - brate life.

Cel-e-brate now, cel-e - brate life. Cel-e-brate now, cel-e - brate life.

D.S. al Coda ⊕ Coda

Cel-e-brate now, cel-e -

Cel-e-brate now, cel-e -

ff

-brate life. Cel - e - brate, cel - e - brate, cel - e - brate, cel - e - brate,

ff

-brate life. Cel - e - brate, cel - e - brate, cel - e - brate, cel - e - brate,

cel - e - brate, cel - e - brate, cel - e - brate, cel - e - brate life!

cel - e - brate, cel - e - brate, cel - e - brate, cel - e - brate life!

125

REPETITION: THE BASIS OF FORM

Motives in Architecture

When architects design buildings they often repeat small units or shapes such as squares, rectangles, circles, or triangles to create a much larger form. Identify some of the small units used to create the buildings pictured here.

Below, the chapel at the Air Force Academy in Colorado Springs. Right, the Flatiron Building in New York City. Bottom, Habitat, in Montréal, Canada.

Motives in Music

Composers often use repetitions of short musical ideas to develop the form of a composition. These ideas are called *motives*. **A motive** is a short, easily recognized musical unit that keeps its basic identity through many repetitions.

In "Floe" from *Glassworks* by Philip Glass, different motives are used to create a larger form.

- Perform these motives from "Floe" on keyboard, recorder, bells, or guitar.

Motives from "Floe"

(6 times)

1.

(2 times)

2.

(4 times)

3.

(4 times)

4.

- Listen to "Floe" and identify the order in which you hear each motive.

 "Floe" from *Glassworks*, by Philip Glass

- Listen again and perform each motive, with the recording, on keyboard, recorder, bells, or guitar.

127

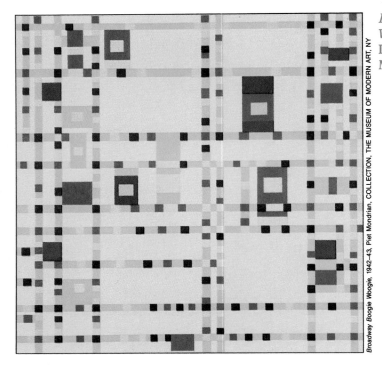

Broadway Boogie Woogie is by the Dutch artist Piet Mondrian.

Broadway Boogie Woogie, 1942–43, Piet Mondrian. COLLECTION, THE MUSEUM OF MODERN ART, NY

Motives in Art

The use of motives is found in many art forms. The two works shown on this page both use repetition of small forms to create a much larger form. The first, *Broadway Boogie Woogie,* by Piet Mondrian, was inspired by the artist's viewing of the traffic on Broadway from his studio in a nearby skyscraper. He compared the cars and trucks to the rhythms of boogie-woogie. The second work is a piece of computer art. What shape or form serves as a motive for this work?

Philip Glass and Minimalism

The contemporary composer Philip Glass was born in Baltimore in 1937. Like many composers, he had a traditional musical education. However, he is most noted for his music in the twentieth-century style called **minimalism.**

While studying music in Europe, Glass met the great Indian sitar player Ravi Shankar, who introduced him to Indian classical music. Later, Glass traveled to Morocco and India to study Eastern music first hand. The influence of Eastern music ultimately was reflected in his own music. While he worked to perfect his style back in the United States, Glass took a variety of jobs, including moving furniture, doing carpentry, and driving a cab. About the same time, he met several painters and sculptors who influenced his work. Their method was to emphasize one aspect of visual art (for example, color or texture) to create the greatest possible effect with the least possible means. Glass adapted this method to his music, in combination with characteristics of the Eastern music he had studied.

Minimalist music does not imitate the sound of Eastern music. However, it does contain some of the same techniques, such as repetition of short rhythmic and melodic patterns. This emphasis on repetition is the basis of all minimalist music. In contrast, other Western musical styles emphasize melody or harmony. Young audiences in particular have found Glass's blend of rock realism and Eastern mysticism appealing.

"Floe" is a typical example of the minimalist style. In it, Glass achieves his effects with only a few repeated rhythmic and melodic ideas. By using orchestral instruments—especially the brasses—in unusual ways, Glass creates the tone qualities that are characteristic of minimalist music.

STORY THROUGH SONG

The Ballad

A **ballad** is a narrative poem or song. The ballad is one of the oldest forms of poetry and one of the oldest kinds of music. Its beginnings are almost impossible to trace, partly because the earliest composers of ballads probably could not read or write. The ballad form apparently was established by 1400. Ballads were passed down by word of mouth from generation to generation. European settlers brought their ballads to the New World, besides composing new ones. Some surviving ballads from the 1500s and 1600s were sung in much the same way as we sing them now.

In his ballad "The Wreck of the Edmund Fitzgerald," the composer and singer Gordon Lightfoot tells of the sinking of a giant ore carrier. Seven different verses, all set to repetitions of the same melody and harmony, describe the loss of the *Edmund Fitzgerald* and her twenty-nine crew members in a raging Lake Superior storm in November 1976.

"The Wreck of the Edmund Fitzgerald" is a ballad set in *strophic form*. **Strophic form** repeats the same melody or section of music with each new verse or stanza of text.

- Listen to "The Wreck of the Edmund Fitzgerald" and follow the story.

 "The Wreck of the Edmund Fitzgerald," by Gordon Lightfoot

- Perform the melodic accompaniment to "The Wreck of the Edmund Fitzgerald" on keyboard, recorder, or bells.

The Wreck of the Edmund Fitzgerald

Words and music by
Gordon Lightfoot

1. The leg - end lives on from the Chip - pe - wa on down of the
With a load of iron ore twenty-six thou - sand tons more than the

big lake they called "Git - chee Gu - mee."
Ed - mund Fitz - ger - ald weighed emp - ty,

The lake, it is said, nev - er___ gives up her dead when the
that good ship and true was a___ bone to be chewed when the

skies of No - vem - ber turn gloom - y.___
"Gales of No - vem - ber" came ear - ly.___

song continues on next page

131

2. ≋

The ship was the pride of the American side
coming back from some mill in Wisconsin.
As the big freighters go it was bigger than most
with a crew and good captain well seasoned,
concluding some terms with a couple of steel firms
when they left fully loaded for Cleveland.
And later that night when the ship's bell rang,
could it be the north wind they'd been feelin'?

3. ≋

The wind in the wires made a tattletale sound
and a wave broke over the railing.
And ev'ry man knew as the captain did too
'twas the witch of November come stealin'.
The dawn came late and the breakfast had to wait
when the Gales of November came slashin'.
When afternoon came it was freezin' rain
in the face of a hurricane west wind.

4. ≋

When suppertime came the old cook came on deck
sayin', "Fellas, it's too rough t' feed ya."
At seven P.M. a main hatchway caved in;
he said, "Fellas, it's bin good t' know ya!"
The captain wired in he had water comin' in
and the good ship and crew was in peril.
And later that night when 'is lights went outta sight
came the wreck of the Edmund Fitzgerald.

5. ≋

Does anyone know where the love of God goes
when the waves turn the minutes to hours?
The searchers all say they'd have made Whitefish Bay
if they'd put fifteen more miles behind 'er.
They might have split up or they might have capsized;
they may have broke deep and took water.
And all that remains is the faces and the names
of the wives and the sons and the daughters.

6. ≋

Lake Huron rolls, Superior sings
in the rooms of her ice-water mansion.
Old Michigan steams like a young man's dreams;
the islands and bays are for sportsmen.
And farther below Lake Ontario
takes in what Lake Erie can send her,
and the iron boats go as the mariners all know
with the Gales of November remembered.

7. ≋

In a musty old hall in Detroit they prayed,
in the "Maritime Sailors' Cathedral."
The church bell chimed 'til it rang twenty-nine times
for each man on the Edmund Fitzgerald.
The legend lives on from the Chippewa on down
of the big lake they call "Gitchee Gumee."
"Superior," they said, "never gives up her dead
when the Gales of November come early!"

132

GORDON LIGHTFOOT

Canadian singer Gordon Lightfoot was born in 1938 in Ontario. His first musical experience was singing in his church choir. He went to Westlake College of Music in Los Angeles where he studied music theory. He later learned to play the guitar and began to experiment with folk music. It was Bob Dylan's socially conscious music that inspired Lightfoot to write and record his first album, *Lightfoot*.

Lightfoot has enjoyed widespread popularity as a singer and guitarist since the early 1970s with tuneful, easy-to-sing hits such as "Sundown" and "If You Could Read My Mind." His clear, warm voice is the perfect vehicle for his ballads about everyday people and their lives. Lately he has concentrated on writing collections of songs illustrating and praising Canadian life. Like the masterful epic "The Wreck of the Edmund Fitzgerald," most of Lightfoot's songs feature only guitar and voice, allowing him to emphasize the story line and mood.

133

An Art Song

The art song was one of the most important forms of the romantic period. These songs usually combine a solo voice with piano accompaniment. Through poetry and music, art songs express a particular mood or idea, often with deep emotion. Like "The Wreck of the Edmund Fitzgerald," *"Schwanenlied"* (shvän' en-lēd) is in strophic form. *"Schwanenlied"* was composed by Fanny Mendelssohn Hensel. The text was written by Heinrich Heine (hīn' riKH hī' nə) (1797–1856), one of the greatest German poets.

● Listen to *"Schwanenlied,"* and read the English translation of the German text on page 135. Decide on a word to describe the mood of the text.

"Schwanenlied," by Fanny Mendelssohn Hensel

Fanny Mendelssohn Hensel (1805–1847), German composer and pianist, was the oldest of four children in an extremely talented family. Her grandfather was a well-known philosopher, and her brother Felix also became a renowned composer and pianist. Fanny displayed great musical talent at an early age. Felix often remarked that she was a better pianist than he was. He always asked her advice on his musical ideas before writing them down.

Fanny Mendelssohn Hensel

Fanny published only five collections of songs and a piano trio during her lifetime. In fact, her early works were published under Felix's name. Queen Victoria's favorite Mendelssohn song, *"Italien,"* actually was written by Fanny. Her art songs, such as *"Schwanenlied,"* reveal many characteristics of the romantic period, such as direct expression of emotions and long, complex melodies.

Schwanenlied (Swan's Song)

Verse 1

Es fällt ein Stern herunter aus seiner funkelnden Höh,
A star falls down from its sparkling heights.

das ist der Stern der Liebe, den ich dort fallen seh.
That is the star of love that I see falling.

Es fallen von Apfelbaume, der weissen Blätter so viel,
So many white leaves fall from the apple tree

es kommen die neckenden Lüfte, und treiben damit ihr spiel.
The teasing breezes come and playfully use them for their games.

Verse 2

Es singt der Schwan im Weiher, und rudert auf und ab,
The swan sings in the pond and glides back and forth,

und immer leiser singend, taucht er ins Fluthengrab.
And ever so softly singing he dips into the deep watery grave.

Es ist so still und dunkel, verweht ist Blatt und Blüth,
It is so still and dark, leaves and blossoms have disappeared.

der Stern ist knisternd zerstoben, Verklungen das Schwanenlied.
The star's brilliance is gone. The swan's song has died away.

Which of these musical characteristics express the mood of
"Schwanenlied"?

slow or fast   major or minor   mostly loud or mostly soft

JUST CHECKING

See how much you remember. Listen to the recording.

1. Listen to the steady beat and perform these motives on keyboard, recorder, bells, or guitar.

2. Perform this melodic accompaniment on bells, recorder or keyboard.

3. Perform this melodic accompaniment on keyboard, bells, or recorder.

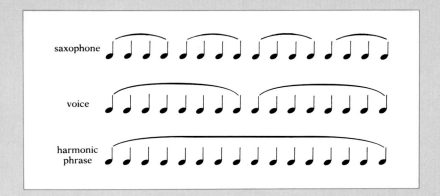

4. Listen to a portion of "The Wreck of the Edmund Fitzgerald" and determine if the form is strophic or ternary.

5. Listen to a portion of "(Life Is a) Celebration" and show the regular and irregular phrase structure by moving your hand in an arc.

6. Listen to *"Schwanenlied"* and decide whether the composition is in major or minor.

7. Show the three phrase lengths in "Careless Whisper" by moving your hands in an arc from left to right.

saxophone

voice

harmonic phrase

8. Name some musical characteristics that express the mood of *"Schwanenlied."*

9. Listen to a portion of "The Wreck of the Edmund Fitzgerald" and determine if the song is in major or minor.

UNIT 7

ELEMENTS
OF FORM

View from Wind River Mountains, Wyoming, Albert Bierstadt, THE MUSEUM OF FINE ARTS, Boston

139

REPETITION IN MUSIC

Identifying Motives

The second movement of Ludwig van Beethoven's Symphony No. 7 is based on repetition of rhythmic and melodic motives.

- Perform these rhythmic motives by patting the quarter notes, pat-sliding the tied notes, clapping the eighth notes, and snapping the triplets with alternating hands.

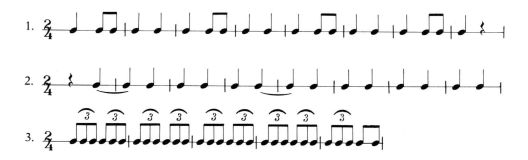

Each of the following melodies uses one of the rhythmic motives you have performed.

- Identify the melody that uses rhythmic motive 1, motive 2, and motive 3.

- Listen and match the rhythmic motives 1, 2, or 3 with recorded examples a, b, and c from the second movement of the Seventh Symphony.

 Beethoven Seventh Motive Montage

Which of the melodies in the Beethoven Seventh Motive Montage sounded smooth and connected?

Which of the melodies sounded detached and crisp?

Music that sounds smooth is said to be performed **legato** (le-gä′ tō). Music that sounds detached and crisp is said to be performed **staccato** (stä-kä′ tō). Notes to be played or sung staccato are written this way: ♩ or ♩ .

Symphony orchestras often consist of over a hundred musicians. These two photos show the Boston Symphony Orchestra in performance.

Identifying Motives in a Listening Map

- Listen to the first portion of the second movement of Beethoven's Symphony No. 7. When you hear rhythmic motive 1 (♩ ♫ | ♩ ♩), find it on the map.

- Examine the map. Find rhythmic motive 2 (♪ ♩ | ♩ ♩) and rhythmic motive 3 (♫♪ ♫♪).
- Follow the map as you listen to the second movement of Beethoven's Symphony No. 7.

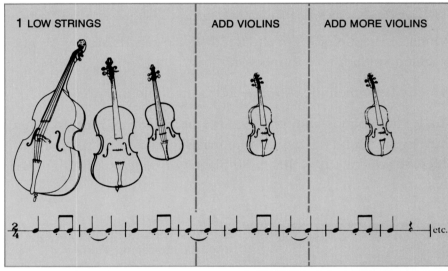

| INTRODUCTION WOODWINDS | 1 LOW STRINGS | ADD VIOLINS | ADD MORE VIOLINS |

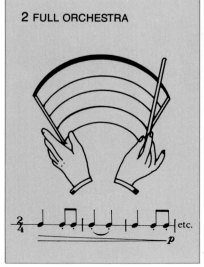

2 FULL ORCHESTRA

3 WOODWINDS: MELODY
STRINGS: ACCOMPANIMENT

WITH

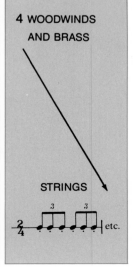

4 WOODWINDS
AND BRASS

STRINGS

5 STRING BASSES: MELODY (PIZZICATO)

WOODWINDS
AND STRINGS:
ACCOMPANIMENT

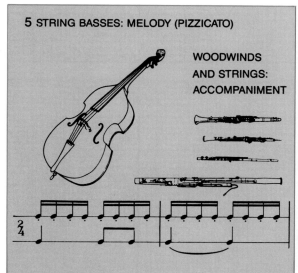

6 POLYPHONY

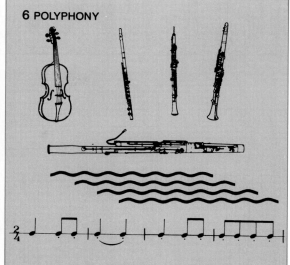

7 FULL ORCHESTRA

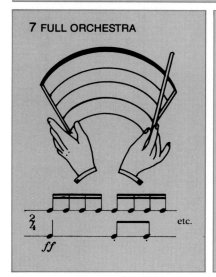

etc.

ff

8 WOODWINDS: MELODY

STRINGS: ACCOMPANIMENT

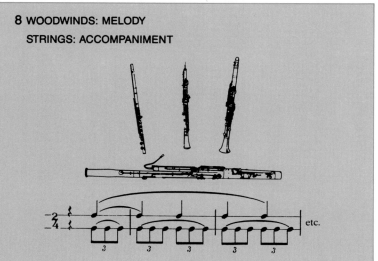

etc.

9 CODA

STRINGS (PIZZICATO) AND

WOODWINDS   WITH

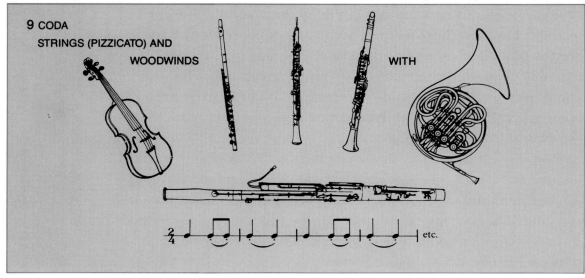

etc.

143

Artists of the classical period often depicted scenes of ancient Greece and Rome.

Countryside of Arcadia, Nicolas Poussin, LOUVRE, Paris

The Classical Period (1750-1830)

The characteristics of music from the classical period are charm, delicacy, and gracefulness. Melodies generally are short and tuneful. Beneath this seeming simplicity there are often deeper feelings; however, these feelings are usually understated. A single section of a classical work can have contrasting moods, and dynamic changes include crescendo and decrescendo. Classical composers wrote operas and concertos, as did the earlier baroque composers. They also established some new musical forms, the symphony and the string quartet.

The orchestra of today developed during this period in musical history. Great composers of the classical period include Haydn (hī′ dən) and Mozart (mōt′ särt). Early works of Beethoven are often considered to be classical in style. However, Beethoven is credited by most musicians with ushering in the next great period in musical history, the romantic period.

Characteristics of Classical Period Music

Changes of mood within
sections of a composition
Dynamic changes including
crescendo and decrescendo
Short, tuneful melodies
Controlled feelings or emotions
Emphasis on unity and balance

The Pantheon, Paris

Hippocrates Refusing the Presents of Artaxerxes, Anne-Louis Girodet-Trioson, FACULTÉ DE MEDECINE, Paris

Above, architects of the classical period often were influenced by Greek and Roman styles. Left, this painting illustrates a scene from the life of Hippocrates, the ancient Greek "father of medicine."

145

REPETITION AND DEVELOPMENT

Repetition in Art

Arthur Dove's painting *Clouds and Water* is made up of simple curved shapes that are repeated and contrasted. The waves in the water are repeated in the shapes of the mountains and clouds. Contrast is provided by the different colors of the water, land, and sky. The sails on the three boats provide additional contrasts of color and movement. Each area of the painting is an adaptation, expansion, contraction, alteration, or elaboration of a basic curved shape.

• Compare the different shapes and forms in the painting.

Transforming a Musical Idea

Like the artist who painted *Clouds and Water*, a composer may decide to adapt, expand, contract, alter, or elaborate a musical idea. This transformation of a musical idea is known as **development.**

Because the melody of "America" is well known, you can probably remember how different parts of the song sound. This should enable you to explore some of the techniques composers use to develop a musical idea.

- Sing through one verse of "America." Use the lyrics to help you keep track of each measure while you are singing.

America

Words by Samuel F. Smith
Music by Henry Carey

How many times does the rhythmic pattern appear in the song?

The rhythmic pattern you just identified is called a **rhythmic motive.**

- Perform the beginning of "America."

- Create your own rhythmic motives by changing the rhythm of one measure.

You have just altered the rhythm of the melody.

- Perform "America" on keyboard, recorder, or bells.
- Perform measure 1 and then measure 11.

My coun-try from ev - 'ry__

You have just created a **melodic motive** from portions of "America."

- Create your own melodic motives by combining other measures of the song.
- Perform measures 7 and 8, then perform measures 9 and 10.

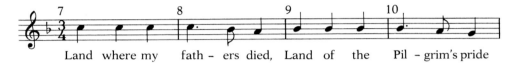

Land where my fath - ers died, Land of the Pil - grim's pride

Do measures 9 and 10 sound higher or lower than measures 7 and 8?

Do they have the same or different rhythm patterns?

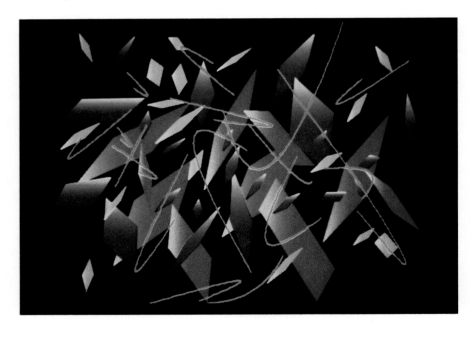

Although the diamond shapes in this computer art are turned at different angles, you can still recognize their basic form.

You can use any of these techniques, along with many others, to develop a musical idea:

        Altering rhythms

        Altering melodies

        Creating rhythmic and melodic motives

Organization in the First Movement of a Symphony

The symphony as a musical art form emerged during the classical period. A **symphony** is a long orchestral work organized into four movements. The first movement is almost always in what is called *sonata allegro form*. **Sonata allegro form** consists of three sections much like ABA form.

The A section sometimes begins with a foreshadowing of the musical ideas to come. This is called the *introduction* and is followed by the presentation of two or more musical ideas or themes. These themes are often contrasting in nature. The presentation of the themes is called the *exposition*. The B section is developmental. Here the themes presented in the exposition are adapted, expanded, contracted, altered, and elaborated. The composer uses a variety of techniques to transform the original musical ideas. The last section of sonata allegro form is the *recapitulation* in which the composer restates each of the themes. This section sometimes ends with a summary called the *coda*.

The following diagram depicts sonata allegro form graphically.

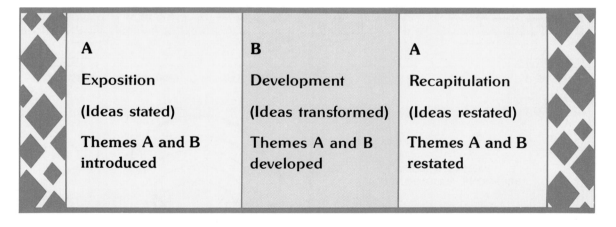

A	B	A
Exposition	Development	Recapitulation
(Ideas stated)	(Ideas transformed)	(Ideas restated)
Themes A and B introduced	Themes A and B developed	Themes A and B restated

Twentieth-century composer Sergei Prokofiev (ser-gā' prō-kof' yəf) (1891–1953) wrote his first symphony in the style of the classical period. The symphony is referred to as **neoclassical** since it exhibits all the characteristics of a classical symphony but was written almost a century after the close of that musical period.

The first movement of Prokofiev's Symphony No. 1 in D Major, or *Classical Symphony,* is an excellent example of sonata allegro form.

- Follow the listening map of the first movement of Prokofiev's *Classical Symphony,* as you listen to the music.

 Classical Symphony, First Movement, by Sergei Prokofiev

EXPOSITION

1 THEME A

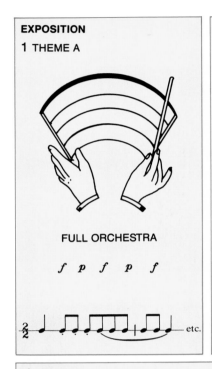

FULL ORCHESTRA

f   p   f   p   f

2 TRANSITION

WOODWINDS AND STRINGS

p   f   p   f

3 INTRODUCTION TO THEME B

WOODWINDS AND STRINGS

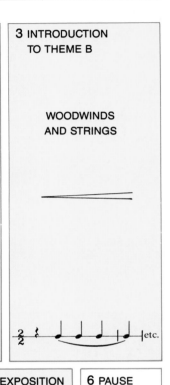

4 THEME B

VIOLINS: MELODY
BASSOONS: ACCOMPANIMENT

MOSTLY *pp*

5 CONCLUSION OF EXPOSITION

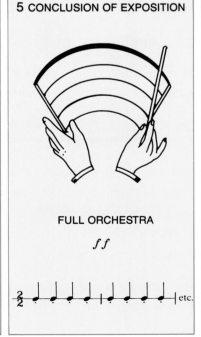

FULL ORCHESTRA

ff

6 PAUSE

DEVELOPMENT
7 DEVELOPMENT OF THEME A IN MINOR

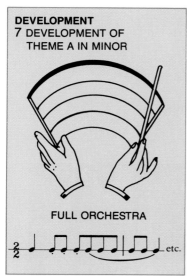

FULL ORCHESTRA

8 DEVELOPMENT OF TRANSITION

WOODWINDS AND STRINGS

f p f

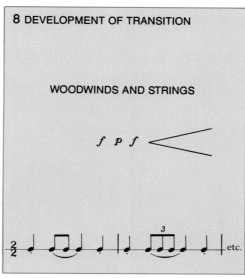

9 DEVELOPMENT OF THEME B

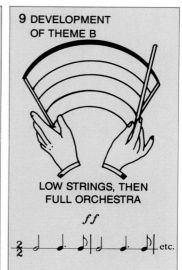

LOW STRINGS, THEN
FULL ORCHESTRA

ff

10 CONCLUSION OF DEVELOPMENT

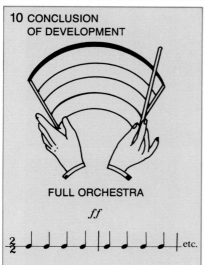

FULL ORCHESTRA

ff

RECAPITULATION
11 THEME A

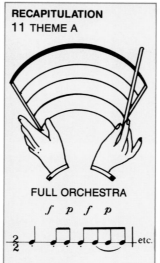

FULL ORCHESTRA

f p f p

12 TRANSITION

WOODWINDS
AND STRINGS

f p f p

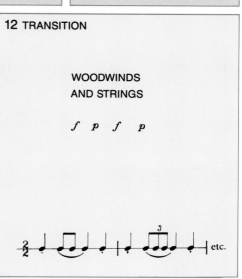

13 INTRODUCTION TO THEME B

WOODWINDS
AND STRINGS

14 THEME B

VIOLINS: MELODY
BASSOONS: ACCOMPANIMENT

MOSTLY *pp*

15 CONCLUSION OF RECAPITULATION

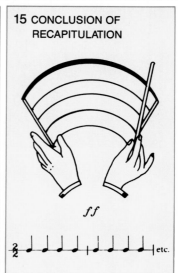

ff

PROGRAM MUSIC

Sounds can be used to convey simple or complex ideas. They can also be organized to depict images or scenes.

- Before listening to music related to one of these scenes, imagine what the music for each picture might sound like.

- Listen to the music and select the scene that is most like the music.

 Program Music Example

The terms below describe some of the musical characteristics of pitch, rhythm, and tone color that helped you select the scene. Which characteristics helped you make your choice?

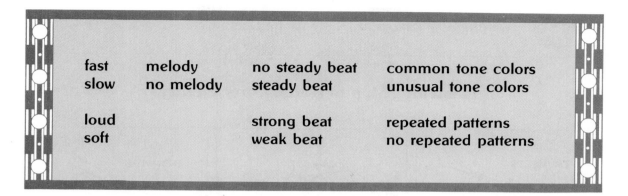

fast	melody	no steady beat	common tone colors
slow	no melody	steady beat	unusual tone colors
loud		strong beat	repeated patterns
soft		weak beat	no repeated patterns

The term *program music* is often used to describe musical works that tell a story, describe an action or event, paint a picture, or create an impression. The term is used in contrast to **absolute music**, music which attempts to do none of those things.

Program music was a popular style of the nineteenth century. People were interested in poetry, prose, mythology, history, and current events. They especially enjoyed hearing musical interpretations of those interests. Composers often used literature or history as a guide for developing their music.

Wellington's Victory by Ludwig van Beethoven is an example of program music that depicts a dramatic battle in 1813 between the French and British armies.

You may recognize three of the main themes in *Wellington's Victory*. The first theme, representing the British army, is "Rule Britannia." This theme is often used in films or on television to represent the British people. The second theme, "Marlborough," represents the French army and is best known to small children as "The Bear Went Over the Mountain." The last popular theme heard is "God Save the King," which uses the same melody as our own patriotic song "America."

• Listen to the three main themes used by Beethoven in *Wellington's Victory*.

 Wellington's Victory Theme Montage

- As you listen to *Wellington's Victory,* follow the listening map. You can determine the losers because the theme representing the defeated army is played in minor and at a soft dynamic level.

Wellington's Victory, by Ludwig van Beethoven

Listening Map to *Wellington's Victory*

1
TRUMPETS

DRUM

2

3
TRUMPETS

DRUM

4

5
TRUMPETS

SOLO

6
FULL ORCHESTRA

7
DRUM

f

FULL
ORCHESTRA

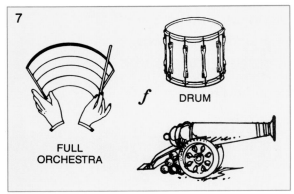

8
WOODWINDS   STRINGS

9

WOODWINDS   STRINGS

10   VICTORY!

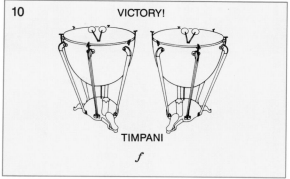

TIMPANI

f

11

"GOD SAVE THE KING"

p

12   VICTORY!

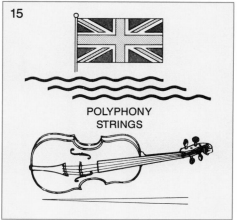

f

13

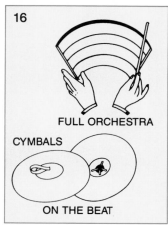

"GOD SAVE THE KING"

$p\ f\ p\ f\ p\ f\ p\ f\ p\ f\ p\ f$

14   STRINGS

FRENCH
HORN

OBOE

so

mi   fa

15

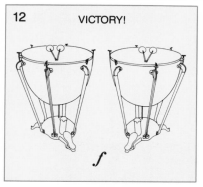

POLYPHONY
STRINGS

16

FULL ORCHESTRA

CYMBALS

ON THE BEAT

17

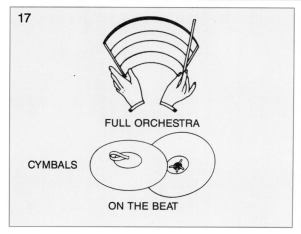

FULL ORCHESTRA

CYMBALS

ON THE BEAT

18

STRINGS, THEN

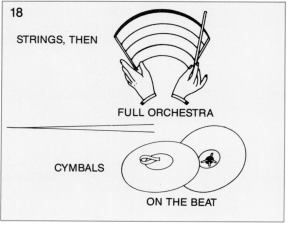

FULL ORCHESTRA

CYMBALS

ON THE BEAT

155

CREATIVITY IN THE TWENTIETH CENTURY

Creativity in Art

The creative principles of balance, unity, control, and variety were extremely important during the baroque, classical, and romantic periods. Some artists of the twentieth century have continued the traditions of the past. To others creativity has been characterized by a search for new ideas and new sounds.

• Examine the contemporary works of art pictured on these pages. Which works illustrate the experimentation of the twentieth century? Which works illustrate the principles emphasized during earlier style periods?

Street View, James Valerio, FRUMKIN/ADAMS GALLERY, NY, Collection of Dr. Larry and Marlene Milner

Artists of the twentieth century have created art in many styles. The painting above is by the American artist James Valerio. The sculpture at right is by the English artist Henry Moore.

Family Group, Henry Moore, THE TATE GALLERY, London

156

Three Musicians, Pablo Picasso, PHILADELPHIA MUSEUM OF ART

Pablo Picasso painted *Three Musicians* (left) in 1921. Joseph Cornell created his "pantry ballet" just for fun.

A Pantry Ballet (for Jacques Offenbach), Joseph Cornell, THE NELSON-ATKINS MUSEUM OF ART, Kansas City, MO

A Composition in Free Form

"A Marvelous Place" is a composition for speaking chorus. The score for this composition looks unusual because it is in *free form*. A composition is in **free form** when the order of the individual sections of the piece can change from one performance to the next. "A Marvelous Place" contains six events that can be performed in any order.

- Examine the score and identify the six events which can change.
- Listen to the recording and follow the score to get ready to perform this composition.

"A Marvelous Place"

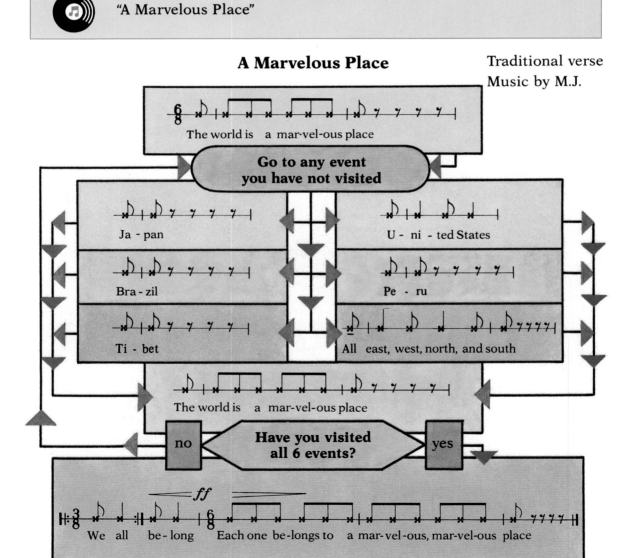

A Marvelous Place

Traditional verse
Music by M.J.

repeat gradually louder until all parts are performing

Creating Free Compositions

Free composition is not new. Composers in different style periods have experimented with giving up their power to make decisions about melody, harmony, tone color, and form. In 1751, William Hayes, an English composer, wrote *The Art of Composing Music by a Method Entirely New, Suited to the Meanest Capacity*. He described a method in which a small paint brush is dipped in ink. The brush then is shaken over music paper so that the ink falls on the staff lines. The ink splatterings then become the note heads. The classical composer Wolfgang Amadeus Mozart created music in which melodies were to be played in an order determined by a spinning dial, such as you see at carnivals.

Here are several suggestions to help you create free compositions. What is free about each of these compositional techniques?

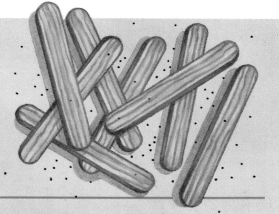

Stick Melody
1. Choose eight pitches.
2. Assign each pitch a number.
3. Number eight sticks.
4. Drop the sticks and read from left to right to determine the order of pitches to be performed.

A	0
B	1
C	2
	⋮
B′	8.
C′	9

Telephone Harmony
1. Choose ten pitches
2. Assign each pitch a number. (0–9)
3. Select 3 ten-digit phone numbers.
4. Write each as a pitch pattern.

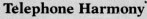
2 1 2 - 7 0 2 - 7 8 9 6
CBC-A′AC-A′B′C′G

5. Perform the three patterns at the same time to produce harmony.

• Combine aspects of both of these free compositional techniques to create music with melody and harmony. Think of other free techniques that can be used to create music.

JUST CHECKING

See how much you remember. Listen to the recording.

1. Listen to the steady beat and perform these rhythm motives by patting the quarter notes, pat-sliding the tied notes, clapping the eighth notes, and snapping the triplets with alternating hands.

2. Identify the melody below that uses rhythm motive 1, motive 2, or motive 3 above.

3. Listen to this section of the second movement of Beethoven's Symphony No. 7 and decide whether the articulation is legato or staccato.

4. Which of the following defines legato? Which defines staccato?

   a. detached and crisp
   b. smooth and connected

5. Listen to this section of the *Classical Symphony,* by **Sergei Prokofiev.**
   Identify the different sections of the exposition section by
   pointing to the descriptions on the listening map.

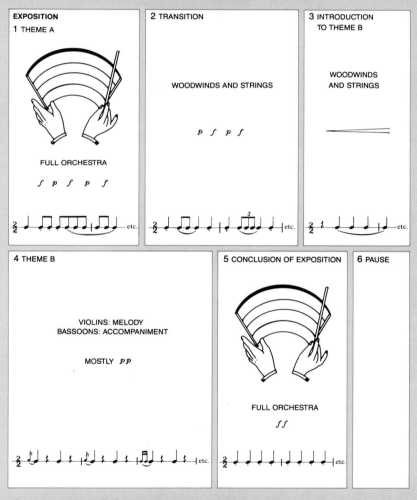

6. Listen to this version of the "America" melody. It is an example of:

           alteration of rhythm   creating a motive

7. Which of the following describes free form?

   a. order of sections can change b. order stays the same

UNIT 8

TONE COLOR IN DIFFERENT STYLES

Guitar, Paris (1912, early), Pablo Picasso. COLLECTION, THE MUSEUM OF MODERN ART, NY

163

Creating Sounds

Musicians have often explored new ways to create sound. Twentieth-century musicians have continued to experiment with tone color. They have developed new instruments. They have also experimented with unusual ways to play traditional instruments. The musicians in these pictures are creating new tone colors.

- Listen to these examples of traditional instruments producing musical sounds in new ways.

"Tone Color Montage"

Percussion Instruments

Percussion instruments are among the oldest musical instruments in the world. Ancient writings, drawings, carvings, and sculptures show percussion instruments in a variety of settings.

Percussion instruments are generally used to establish or maintain the beat. Many musical compositions feature strong, repeated rhythms on percussion instruments.

- Read and practice each pattern with your drumsticks using the matched grip. Use your right hand (R) and left hand (L) as indicated.

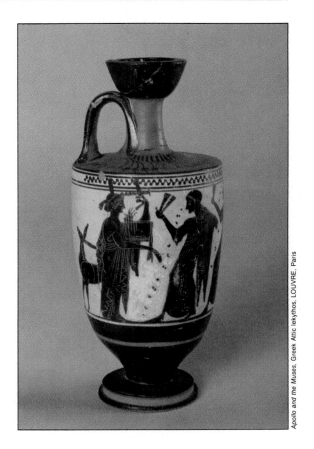

This Greek vase is about twenty-five hundred years old. The god of music, Apollo, is shown at left. The woman at right is playing an ancient percussion instrument.

A 4/4 R L R L R R L R R L R L R L R L R R L R

B 4/4 R R L R R L R R L R R L

C 4/4 RLRLRLRLR L RLRLRLRLR L RLRLRLRLR L RLRLRLRLR

D 4/4 RLRLRLRLR R L RLRLRLRLR R L RLRLRLRLR R L RLRLRLRLR

165

Performing a Rhythmic Accompaniment

Vangelis (van-je′ lis), a Greek composer, created the theme music for the Academy Award-winning film *Chariots of Fire*. The rhythms you have performed can be played as an accompaniment to *Heaven and Hell*, Part 2, another of his compositions.

- Listen to the recording of *Heaven and Hell*, Part 2. Read and perform the rhythmic accompaniment with your drumsticks using the matched grip.

 Heaven and Hell, Part 2 by Vangelis

Accompaniment to *Heaven and Hell*, Part 2

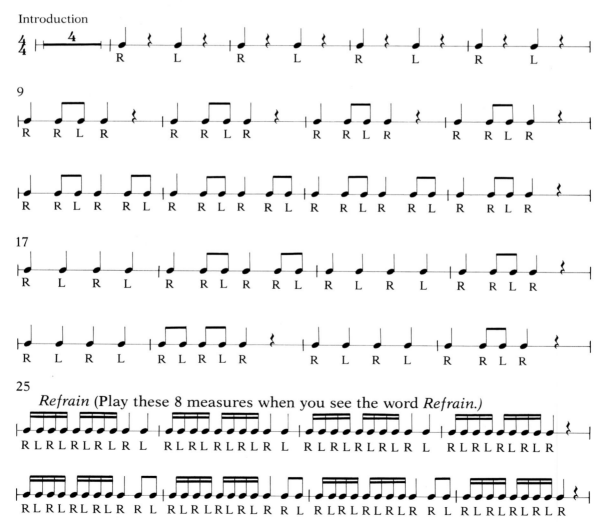

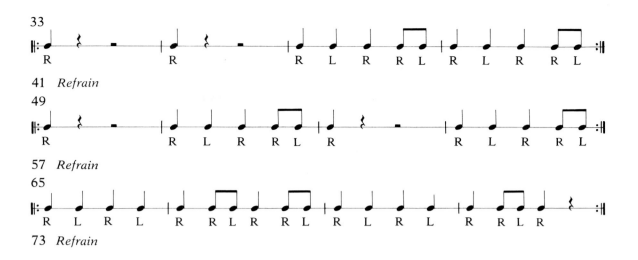

41 *Refrain*

49

57 *Refrain*

65

73 *Refrain*

The Greek composer Vangelis was born in Athens in 1943. He is basically a self-taught musician. As a child he studied the piano and later the pipe organ. His interest in the variety of sounds that could be produced by the pipe organ led Vangelis to its modern equivalent, the synthesizer. The possibilities of producing both traditional and non-traditional sounds attracted him.

Vangelis performed with the Greek rock band Formynx. Political pressures led him to leave Greece and settle in Paris. He composed soundtracks for many European films and television documentaries.

The synthesizer has enabled Vangelis to use many new sounds. He finds this instrument the best means of expressing his musical ideas. He has composed, produced, and performed on over forty record albums.

New Percussion Sounds

Sometimes percussionists use their instruments in new or different ways. In this example, the drumsticks are used in different ways to create new tone colors. The symbol 𝄪 means "hold the drumsticks in the air and tap them lightly together." The symbol 🅇→ means "hold the drumsticks in the air, tap them together, then slide one over the other as shown in this photograph."

• Read and practice these patterns with your drumsticks.

• Perform these patterns as you listen to *Heaven and Hell*, Part 2 again. Use this order:

A–B–C–D–E–D–E–D–C–D

Notation

The tone colors of "Misty, Moisty Morning" are produced by using traditional instruments in new ways. The composer used some special notation to indicate these new sounds.

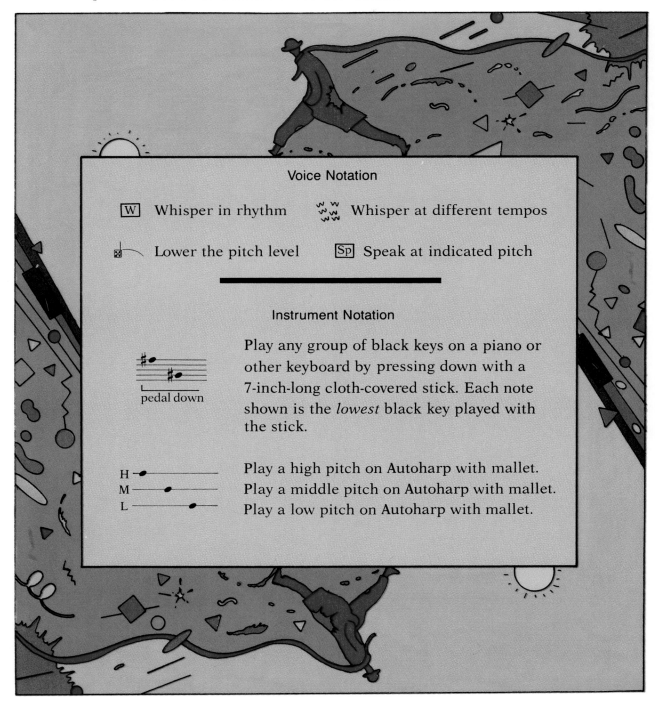

Voice Notation

| W | Whisper in rhythm | Whisper at different tempos |
| Lower the pitch level | Sp | Speak at indicated pitch |

Instrument Notation

pedal down — Play any group of black keys on a piano or other keyboard by pressing down with a 7-inch-long cloth-covered stick. Each note shown is the *lowest* black key played with the stick.

H — Play a high pitch on Autoharp with mallet.
M — Play a middle pitch on Autoharp with mallet.
L — Play a low pitch on Autoharp with mallet.

- Perform "Misty, Moisty Morning" to experience music with new
  tone colors.

Misty, Moisty Morning

Traditional text
Music by M.J.

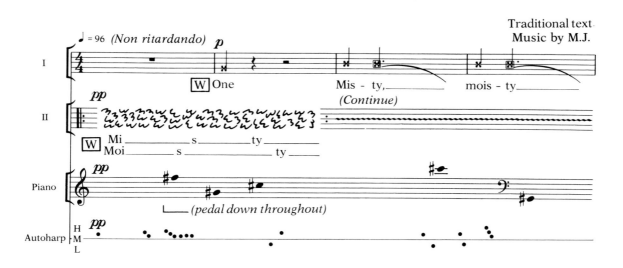

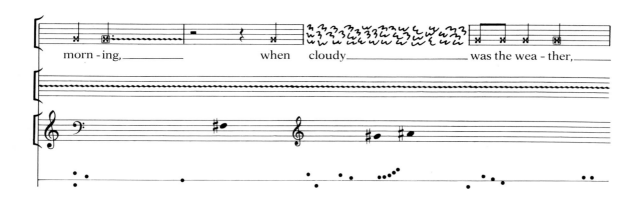

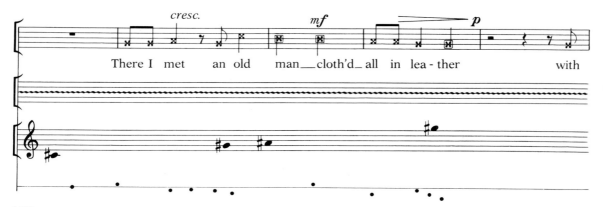

cap un-der his chin. "How do you do?"_____ And "How do you_

_ do?" [Sp] a-gain. [W] Mis - ty,___mois - ty ___morn - ing.___

Other New Tone Colors

Krzysztof Penderecki (kris' tof pen-de-re' skē) is a contemporary
Polish composer who draws novel sounds from voices and
traditional instruments. He also was one of the first composers to
experiment with sounds such as saws cutting wood and paper
rustling, as well as unusual vocal effects. His *Saint Luke Passion*
was an immediate success after its premiere in 1966.

- Listen to part of the *Saint Luke Passion*. Listen for singers
  hissing, shouting, and whispering, and for percussive effects
  produced by voices in the chorus.

 Saint Luke Passion by Krzysztof Penderecki

FROM PIPE ORGAN TO SYNTHESIZER

Pipe Organ

During the baroque period (1600–1750) the pipe organ was a popular instrument. It could produce a wide variety of sounds.

- Listen for the sound of the pipe organ.

 Toccata and Fugue in D Minor, by Johann Sebastian Bach

Pipe Organ

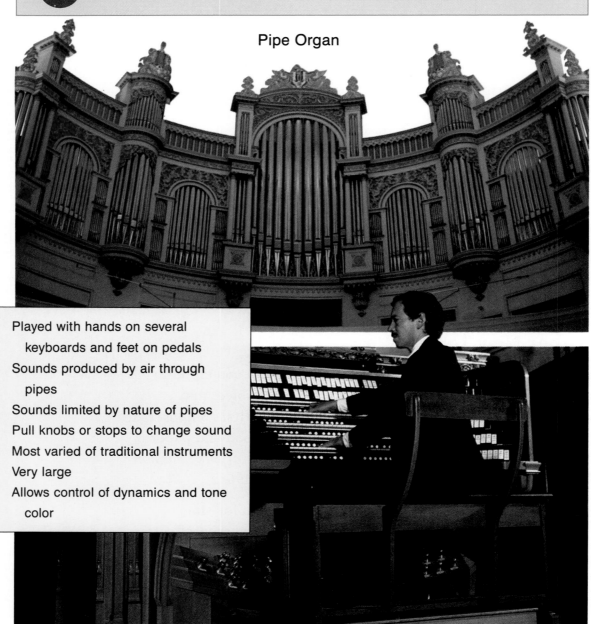

Played with hands on several
  keyboards and feet on pedals
Sounds produced by air through
  pipes
Sounds limited by nature of pipes
Pull knobs or stops to change sound
Most varied of traditional instruments
Very large
Allows control of dynamics and tone
  color

Synthesizer

The Greek composer Vangelis first composed for the pipe organ. He later became interested in the synthesizer because of its even greater tone color possibilities. He composed "Alpha," from his *Albedo 39,* for the synthesizer.

• Listen and describe the traditional and nontraditional sounds.

 "Alpha," from *Albedo 39,* by Vangelis

Ensembles for Synthesizer takes advantage of other tone color possibilities.

• Listen for the many sounds of the synthesizer.

 Ensembles for Synthesizer by Milton Babbitt

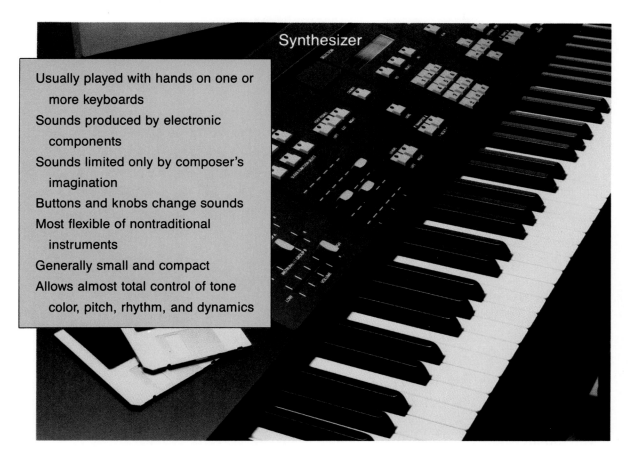

Synthesizer

Usually played with hands on one or
  more keyboards
Sounds produced by electronic
  components
Sounds limited only by composer's
  imagination
Buttons and knobs change sounds
Most flexible of nontraditional
  instruments
Generally small and compact
Allows almost total control of tone
  color, pitch, rhythm, and dynamics

Moving to Sounds of the Twentieth Century

These pictures show contemporary dance movements.

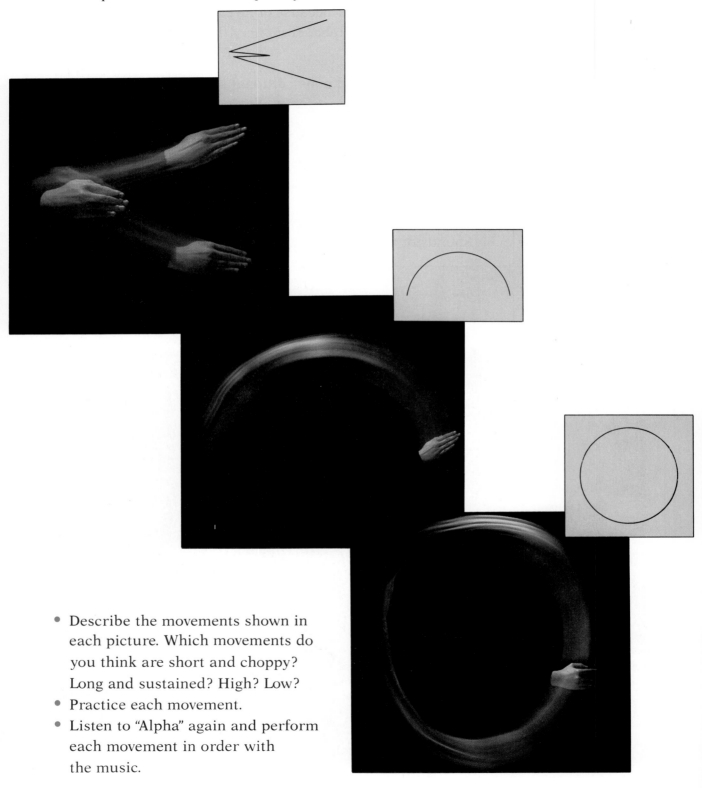

- Describe the movements shown in each picture. Which movements do you think are short and choppy? Long and sustained? High? Low?
- Practice each movement.
- Listen to "Alpha" again and perform each movement in order with the music.

174

NEW SOUNDS FROM A FAMILIAR INSTRUMENT

What Is It?

Sometimes familiar instruments can produce new or different tone colors.

● Listen to this music. Try to identify the instrument or instruments you hear.

 The Perilous Night, by John Cage

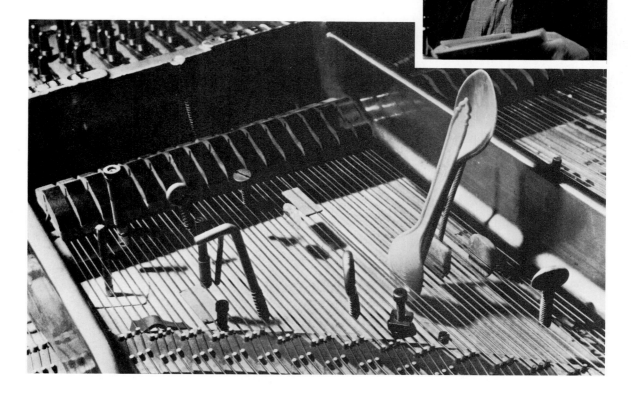

The instrument you heard is a **prepared piano.** Pianos can be prepared in several ways. Items made of wood, metal, or rubber can be placed on or between the strings of the piano. Other piano sounds are produced when the performer strums the strings inside the piano or uses a mallet to hit the wood of the piano. It all depends what sounds the composer wants produced.

John Cage, an American composer, developed the idea of the prepared piano and used it in his compositions to produce different tone colors.

Inside the Piano

A piano has many parts: keyboard, pedals, hammers, strings.
You can look inside a piano to see how the parts work together.

- Observe the hammers. What do they do?

- Place your hand across a group of strings. Play the keys for these strings. What happens to the tone?

- The thickness of the strings and the number of strings related to each key affect the sound produced by the key. Locate the thickest strings. What kind of tone do their keys produce?

- Locate the keys that use three strings; two strings; one string. What kind of tones do these keys produce?

- Find the pedals. What is the purpose of each?

Performing on a Prepared Piano

"Eraser Piano Tees" is a prepared piano composition written for eight prepared notes.

- Prepare four low notes on the piano by using two large rubber erasers. Place each eraser between two sets of low strings.

- Prepare four middle range notes (near middle C) by using four golf tees. Place each tee between the two strings for each middle range note.

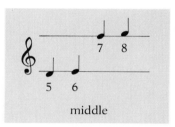

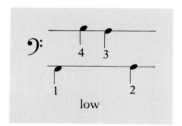

- Use your prepared piano notes to play this composition. The pitches are numbered from the lowest to highest.

Eraser Piano Tees

Dorothy Gail Elliott

THE ELECTRONIC REVOLUTION

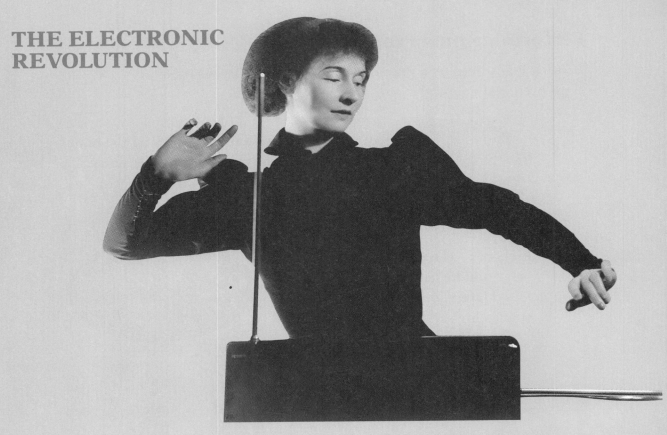

Electronic Musical Instruments

Electronic musical instruments were developed in the twentieth century. In 1927 Leon Theremin (ther′ e-min), a Russian musician, invented the first electronic musical instrument, the Theremin. To control the pitch, the player moves his or her hands toward or away from vertical and horizontal antennas. In 1928 Maurice Martenot (mär-te-nô′), a French musician, invented the Ondes Martenot (ônd′ mär-te-nô′), the ancestor of the synthesizer.

At top, Theremin players must wear special tight-fitting clothes. Even the rustle of fabric will change the pitch of the Theremin. Above, synthesizers include many electronic components.

The electronic revolution moved quickly in music. By the late 1950s, many studios for electronic music were in operation. They were equipped with sound generators, filters, mixers, and recorders.

With the invention of the transistor and then the integrated circuit the technology to create and manipulate electronic sound became easier to use and less expensive. Synthesizers, units that combined sound generators, sound modifiers and a keyboard in a single control system appeared. The Moog and Buchla synthesizers were complete electronic studios. Today simplified units are available to the general public at moderate prices.

Above, the Moog synthesizer was developed by Robert Moog in the 1960s. Below left, Tomita has created electronic versions of much "classical" music.

One Composition — Several Styles

Pictures at an Exhibition by Modest Mussorgsky was composed for the piano alone. The French composer Maurice Ravel arranged the work for full orchestra. In 1975, the Japanese composer Isao Tomita created an electronic version.

- Listen to "Promenade" from *Pictures at an Exhibition* in piano, orchestral, and electronic versions. Compare. In which version is the contrast of dynamics and tone color most obvious? Which version do you find most interesting? Why?

 "Promenade Montage"

More Electronic Music

Milton Babbitt has long been a composer of electronic music.
His control of sound is evident in *Composition for Synthesizer*,
composed in 1960–1961. The synthesizer produces pitches and
rhythms from directions provided by the composer. This work
presents sounds with an evenness and a speed only possible
through electronics.

 Composition for Synthesizer, by Milton Babbitt

As you listen to this composition follow this description:
1. Two gonglike sustained chords. A staccato melody.
2. Two sustained chords. Two staccato melodies.
3. One sustained chord. Two high staccato melodies with a low,
   legato melody.

Milton Babbitt, distinguished contemporary American composer, was born in
Philadelphia in 1916. He received his
early musical training in Jackson, Mississippi, and went on to study at New York
University and Princeton University. He
later became a professor of music at Princeton, where he also taught mathematics.

Babbitt began a program of electronic music at Princeton and Columbia
universities, working with the newly developed synthesizer. He
helped create the Columbia–Princeton Electronic Music Center,
which became a haven for experiments in electronic music. Babbitt
has also written many books and articles on music and musicians.
His theories about mathematics and music and his innovations
with the synthesizer have influenced the musical thinking of many
young American composers.

RECYCLING FOR SOUND

Found Objects

Composers sometimes search for new sound sources when traditional musical instruments are not able to produce all the sounds that they want. *Suite for Percussion*, by Lou Harrison, uses both traditional percussion instruments and new sound sources. His new sources include **found objects**, or everyday objects.

- Listen for both traditional instruments and found objects you think were used.

Suite for Percussion, by Lou Harrison

Your Own Recycled Sound Composition

You and your classmates can create your own compositions using new sources for sound. It is more fun to work in small groups.

1. Work with your group to identify classroom objects (found objects) that would be good sound sources.
2. Experiment with your new instruments. Discover one short sound and one sustained sound.
3. To create unity, play one instrument continuously throughout the composition.
4. Plan a definite beginning and a definite ending.
5. Plan a definite order for different players.
6. To create variety, use three or four different instruments for contrast. Use silence, different dynamics, different tempos, and different pitches. Try different combinations.
7. Perform your composition several different ways.
8. Tape-record different performances of your composition.
9. Decide which of your performances demonstrates the most contrast. Which one is the most interesting?

Unusual Instruments

After World War II, the United States Navy left many large, empty oil containers in the West Indies. These fifty-gallon steel containers inspired the people of the West Indies to create their own special instruments. The oil containers were cut and hammered into steel drums. Groups of steel drum players formed bands with their own unique tone color.

- Listen for the tone color of the steel drums as you pat or clap the steady beat.

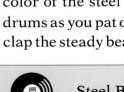 Steel Band Music

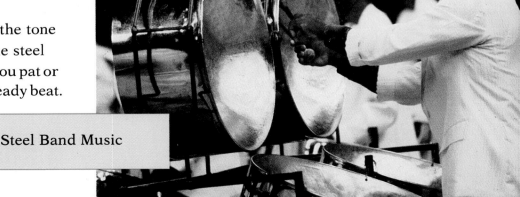

Creating New Instruments

Harry Partch (1901-1973), an American experimental composer, inspired others with his creative ideas. He also invented original instruments for special effects.

- Listen to learn about his composition *Spoils of War* and the unique instruments used in it.

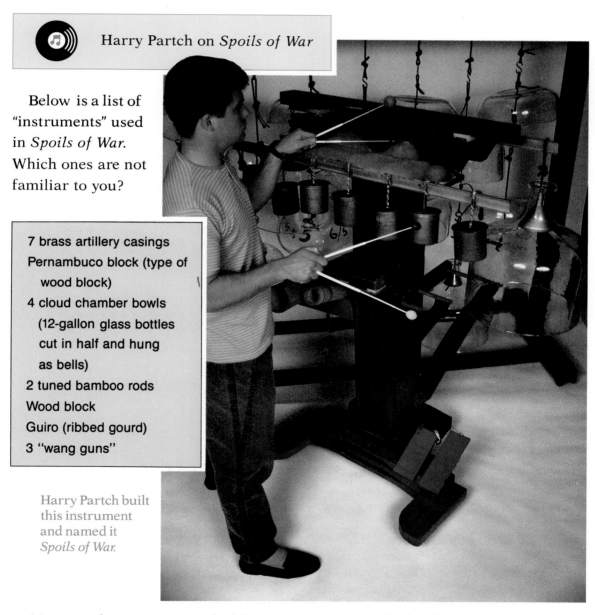

Harry Partch on *Spoils of War*

Below is a list of "instruments" used in *Spoils of War*. Which ones are not familiar to you?

7 brass artillery casings
Pernambuco block (type of
    wood block)
4 cloud chamber bowls
    (12-gallon glass bottles
    cut in half and hung
    as bells)
2 tuned bamboo rods
Wood block
Guiro (ribbed gourd)
3 "wang guns"

Harry Partch built
this instrument
and named it
Spoils of War.

Many modern composers feel free to use any sounds that have the qualities they like. What found instruments might you use to improvise music?

JUST CHECKING

See how much you remember. Listen to the recording.

1. Listen to the steady beat and perform these rhythms on drumsticks using the matched grip.

2. Listen to a portion of the *Saint Luke Passion* and identify the unusual vocal effects.

3. Listen to excerpts of three versions of "Promenade" and describe the contrasts of dynamics and tone color.

4. The unique tone color of this ensemble is produced on homemade instruments. Name the instrument.

5. Perform these vocal sounds with the recording of "Misty, Moisty Morning."

6. Listen to this selection and tell whether the tone color is created by a pipe organ or a synthesizer.

7. Listen to "Alpha" from *Albedo 39* by Vangelis. Use appropriate contemporary dance movements with this piece.

8. Name and describe two unusual instruments or familiar instruments used in unusual ways.

9. Listen and identify the selection you hear. Choose from the titles below.
   a. Toccata and Fugue in D minor
   b. "Alpha" from *Albedo 39*
   c. *Heaven and Hell,* Part 2
   d. "Promenade" from *Pictures at an Exhibition*
   e. *The Perilous Night*

10. Listen to a portion of *The Perilous Night* and describe how the composer used a traditional instrument to produce different tone colors.

11. Listen to a portion of *Spoils of War* and describe several of the original instruments Harry Partch invented.

YEAR-END REVIEW

1. Listen to determine whether the style of each example is African, synth-pop, Japanese, calypso, or reggae.

2. Listen to "Elements" and determine whether the form of the selection is AB or ABA.

3. Listen to this musical selection, which is an example of changing meters. Identify when the meter changes by conducting the appropriate pattern. The selection begins in duple meter.

4. Listen to this excerpt from "Caprice" from Claude Bolling's Suite for Violin and Jazz Piano. Determine if this section is in compound or quadruple meter. Demonstrate your answer by conducting the appropriate pattern.

5a. Play the following pitches on keyboard or bells that make up the twelve-tone row on which the melody of "The Web" is based.

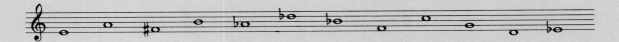

b. Play the retrograde of this tone row on keyboard or bells.

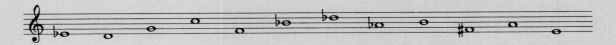

6. Perform this twelve-bar blues harmonic progression on bells or keyboard.

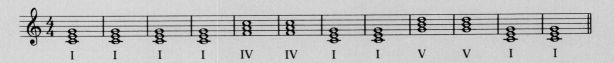

7a. Listen to a section of "Mi Caballo Blanco" and raise your hand when you hear the music modulate.

b. Listen to a section of "Mi Caballo Blanco" and decide if the music modulates to a higher or lower key.

8. Listen to *"Schwanenlied"* and decide whether the composition is in major or minor.

9. Listen to this section of Symphony No. 1 by Sergei Prokofiev. Identify the different parts of the exposition section by pointing to the descriptions on the listening map.

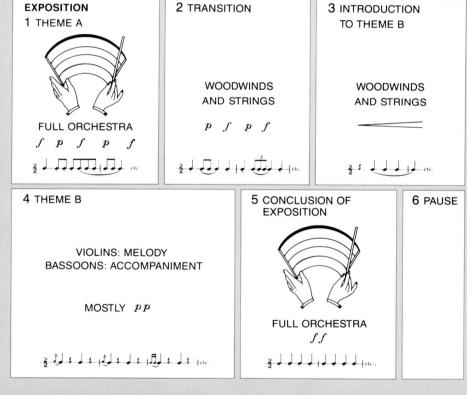

10. Listen and identify the selection you hear. Choose from the titles below.

    a. Toccata and Fugue in D minor

    b. "Alpha"

    c. *Heaven and Hell,* Part 2

    d. "Promenade" *(Pictures at an Exhibition)*

    e. *The Perilous Night*

WESTERN MUSICAL STYLES

Francesco Veracini

Chopin Playing the Piano in Prince Anton Radziwill's Salon at Berlin, Siemiradski

RENAISSANCE

O Care, thou wilt despatch me, by Thomas Weelkes

One of the most popular forms of vocal music in the Renaissance was the **madrigal** (mad′ ri-gəl). Madrigals were written in polyphonic style, usually for five singers. They generally were short works, simple in structure. The lyrics were taken from both great literature and popular poetry. Like the popular songs of today, most madrigals were about love, happy or unhappy. Other topics included politics and issues of the day. Most madrigals were in **strophic** form, with each verse being sung to essentially the same music. This made madrigals easy to learn.

Vocal music was especially popular in the Renaissance, which is often called the "Golden Age of Singing." Church music was sung by professional, all-male choirs, but madrigals were sung by both men and women. Madrigals were performed at social gatherings and as home entertainment. Usually one performer sang each part, sometimes accompanied by recorders, lutes, or viols playing the same music.

In *O Care, thou wilt despatch me,* the English composer Thomas Weelkes looks to music to cheer him up.

> O Care, thou wilt despatch me,
> If music do not match thee.
> Fa la la la la la la.
> So deadly dost thou sting me,
> Mirth only help can bring me.
> Fa la la la la la,
> Fa la la la la la.

- Listen for the two moods the composer portrays. How does the music depict his unhappiness? How does it depict the joy he hopes to find in music?

 O Care, thou wilt despatch me, by Thomas Weelkes

- Compare madrigals with today's pop music. What do both have in common?

During the Renaissance, people enjoyed singing and playing music together. The instruments shown in these paintings include viols (early members of the violin family), lutes, recorder, and a type of portable harpsichord.

Hearing, Abraham Bosse

Group with Lute Player and Three Musicians on the Terrace of a House, unknown 16th-century artist

191

BAROQUE

"Spring" (First Movement) from *The Four Seasons,* by Antonio Vivaldi

The **concerto** (kôn-cher′tō) was one of the most important instrumental forms used in the baroque period. The term *concerto* comes from the Italian word *concertare* (kôn-cher-tä′ re), which suggests a friendly argument or contrasting forces. In a concerto, one instrument or group of instruments is set against the orchestra.

The Four Seasons is a group of violin concertos written around 1725 by the Italian baroque composer Antonio Vivaldi (än-tō′ nē-ō vi-väl′ dē) (1675-1741). Each concerto is accompanied by a poem, also written by Vivaldi, describing that season. This is a very early example of **program music,** music that tells a story or describes a scene.

One of the musical characteristics emphasized in the baroque concerto was *contrast.* In a style typical of the baroque, Vivaldi used two contrasting groups of instruments, contrasting melodies, and abrupt contrasts of loud and soft.

Vivaldi was born in Venice and lived most of his life there. This painting by the Italian artist Canaletto (1697–1768) shows Venice as it looked during Vivaldi's lifetime.

"Spring" begins with the main theme played by everyone. Sections of a concerto played by everyone are called **ritornello** (ri-tôr-ne′ lō). The contrasting sections, called **episodes,** are played by the solo players. The music played suggests musical descriptions of spring, such as birds singing, murmuring waters, lightning and thunder.

192

Each picture represents musical sounds. The term *concertino* (kôn-cher-tē′ no) refers to the solo instrument or instruments. *Tutti* (tōo′ tē) refers to all the instruments together.

● Which pictures are similar? Which are different?

● Listen to "Spring" and notice the contrasts in tone color, themes, and dynamics. Follow the map as you listen.

● Describe the sound of the baroque orchestra. What instruments are used? What keyboard instrument can you hear throughout the concerto?

"Spring" (First Movement), from *The Four Seasons,* by Antonio Vivaldi

Listening Map of "Spring" (First Movement) from *The Four Seasons*

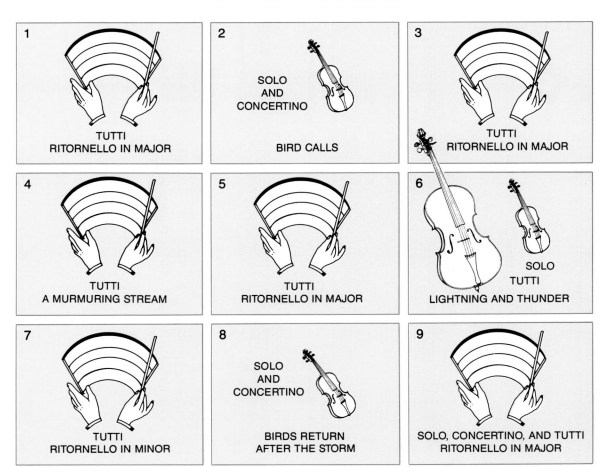

1	2	3
TUTTI RITORNELLO IN MAJOR	SOLO AND CONCERTINO — BIRD CALLS	TUTTI RITORNELLO IN MAJOR

4	5	6
TUTTI A MURMURING STREAM	TUTTI RITORNELLO IN MAJOR	SOLO / TUTTI LIGHTNING AND THUNDER

7	8	9
TUTTI RITORNELLO IN MINOR	SOLO AND CONCERTINO — BIRDS RETURN AFTER THE STORM	SOLO, CONCERTINO, AND TUTTI RITORNELLO IN MAJOR

193

Quintet for Clarinet and Strings in A Major, K. 581, Fourth Movement, by Wolfgang Amadeus Mozart

Compositions for small groups of instruments are called **chamber music** because they are designed to be performed in rooms (chambers) rather than concert halls. Like **symphonies** (works for full orchestra), chamber works are in several movements.

For the fourth and final movement of his Clarinet Quintet, Wolfgang Amadeus Mozart (volf′ gäng ä-mä-dā′ o͞os mōt′ särt) decided to write a theme with six variations and a **coda**, or conclusion. The theme itself is a very simple one, which Mozart varies in several ways. For example, he shows off the instruments' abilities to change from major to minor, or to play **legato** (lā-gä′ tō, smoothly) or **staccato** (stä-kä′ tō, detached). For contrasting tone color, Mozart even leaves out the clarinet entirely in one variation.

• Listen to the music and read the description on page 195. Notice the contrast between staccato and legato sections.

 Quintet for Clarinet and Strings in A Major, K. 581, Fourth Movement, by Wolfgang Amadeus Mozart

1. *Theme:* Cheerful, staccato theme is played and immediately repeated. The second part of the theme, momentarily legato, leads right back to the first (staccato) part, and this is repeated.

2. *Variation 1:* Clarinet, legato, has a new tune as strings play the staccato basic theme. This continues into Part 2 of the theme.

3. *Variation 2:* Strings agitated, but melody soars when clarinet enters. In Part 2 the agitation continues.

4. *Variation 3:* A change to minor gives a melancholy quality to the theme. This entire variation is played by strings only.

5. *Variation 4:* Rapid passages in clarinet accompany a return to the jolly mood of the theme in the strings.

6. *Adagio (Variation 5):* Change to a slow tempo is introduced by a series of chords and descending passages on the clarinet. Strings play yet another variation on the theme, joined by a wistful song on the clarinet, and this segment is repeated. The second part of the theme has the clarinet dominating, then giving in to the strings, and this segment also is repeated. A short, legato passage leads to:

7. *Allegro (Variation 6):* Another treatment of the basic theme. A coda of four chords brings this music to a strong conclusion.

Below, a typical chamber music concert during Mozart's time. Right, the child Mozart (at the keyboard) with his father and sister.

The Concert, Augustin de Saint Aubin

Mozart as a Child, with his Father and Sister, Carmontelle, MUSÉE CONDÉ Chantilly

"Un bel dì vedremo," from *Madama Butterfly,* by Giacomo Puccini

Opera is one of the most exciting of all musical forms, for it offers not only music, but also dramatic action, scenery, costumes, interesting stories and, often, unusual lighting effects. An opera performance, therefore, is a special event.

Madama Butterfly, by the Italian composer Giacomo Puccini, is one of the most popular operas ever written. Puccini's characters are understandable and human.

Madama Butterfly is another name for Cio-Cio-San (chō' chō-sän), a young Japanese woman who marries an American naval officer, Lieutenant Pinkerton. She plans to devote her life to this marriage, but to Pinkerton, it is just a temporary fling until he meets and marries the American woman of his dreams. Butterfly remains true, but Pinkerton, while in America, marries someone else. When Butterfly realizes that Pinkerton has deserted her, she kills herself.

Butterfly sings the famous **aria** (ä' rē-ä, solo song) *"Un bel dì vedremo,"* while she still believes Pinkerton will come back to her. She tells her servant, Suzuki, that one beautiful day Pinkerton will return, and she describes everything she thinks will happen.

The powerful opening melody of this aria occurs again near the end of the song, making a kind of ABA form. Butterfly's belief that Pinkerton will return to her is reflected in the straightforward melody. Near the end of her song, the music becomes more insistent as she talks herself and her servant into believing that what she says actually will come to pass.

As you listen to this selection, you will notice that the composer has provided several changes of mood and tempo to illustrate the situations Butterfly describes. Puccini's melody is strong at the beginning when Pinkerton's return is described, but becomes gentler as Butterfly tells of her own reactions to the situation. She will stay where she is, waiting anxiously for Pinkerton to find her, almost unable to control her emotions. The first melody returns as she describes their first meeting. The aria reaches its peak near the end as Butterfly tries to assure Suzuki that Pinkerton will, indeed, return.

Right, poster advertising a 1906 production of *Madama Butterfly*. Below and page 198, Renata Scotto in the Metropolitan Opera production. Below is the wedding scene; on page 198, *"Un bel dì vedremo."*

- Follow the Italian words and their translation as you hear them. Notice how Puccini's music reflects the hopes and feelings to which Butterfly refers.

Un bel dì, vedremo
Levarsi un fil di fumo
Sull'estremo confin del mare.
E poi la nave appare.
Poi la nave bianca
Entra nel porto,
Romba il suo saluto.
Vedi? È venuto!
Io non gli scendo incontro. Io no. Mi
metto là sul ciglio del colle e aspetto,
e aspetto gran tempo e non mi pesa la
lunga attesa.
E uscito dalla folla cittadina un uomo,
un picciol punto s'avvia per la collina.

Chi sarà? Chi sarà? E come sarà giunto
che dirà? Che dirà? Chiamerà
Butterfly dalla lontana. Io, senza dar
risposta me ne starò nascosta un po'
per celia, e un po' per non morire al
primo incontro, ed egli alquanto in
pena chiamerà, chiamerà: "Piccina
mogliettina olezzo di verbena" i nomi
che mi dava al suo venire.

Tutto questo avverrà, te lo prometto.

Tienti la tua paura, io con sicura fede
l'aspetto.

One fine day, we shall see
A thread of smoke rising
Over the horizon
And then the ship will appear.
Then the white ship
Enters the harbor.
Her salute thunders out.
You see? He has come!
I don't go down to meet him. Not I.
I stand on the brow of the hill and wait,
and wait a long time and do not weary
of the long watch.
Out of the city crowds there comes a
man—a tiny speck—who makes his way
toward the hill.
Who can it be? Who can it be?
And when he arrives what will he say?
What will he say? He will call
Butterfly from the distance. I, without
answering, will stay hidden partly for
fun, and partly so as not to die at the
first meeting. And he, a little troubled,
will call, he will call: "My little wife,
my sweet-scented flower"—the names
he used to call me when he came.
All this will come to pass, I promise you.

Keep your fears: I, with unshakeable
faith, will await him.

 "Un bel dì vedremo," from *Madama Butterfly,* by Giacomo Puccini

Étude in E Minor, Opus 25, No. 5, by Frédéric Chopin

Polish composer Frédéric Chopin specialized in writing music for the piano. Among his finest works, which include waltzes, sonatas, and many other pieces, are his **études**. *Étude* means "study," and an étude's purpose is to help students with technical playing problems. Chopin's études are more than just studies, however, because they are important musical selections in their own right. Chopin played several of them in his concerts, and many pianists do so today.

Of the more than two dozen études that Chopin composed, the Étude in E Minor, Opus 25, No. 5, is particularly impressive. Its opening section (A) is mainly staccato and is played at a fast tempo. The middle section (B) offers an expressive legato, in a slower tempo. When the A section returns, its staccato idea brings to mind the strong contrast that exists between the three sections of this work. Chopin includes a coda (ending section) with chords and a melodic trill at the close.

- Listen to the Étude in E Minor and raise your hand when you hear the contrasting B section.

- How does the étude show unity and variety?

🎵 Étude in E Minor, Opus 25, No. 5, by Frédéric Chopin

Chopin Playing the Piano in Prince Anton Radziwill's Salon at Berlin, Siemiradski

Frédéric Chopin, Eugène Delacroix, LOUVRE, Paris

Chopin often played private concerts in the homes of the nobility.

TWENTIETH CENTURY

Infernal Dance, from *The Firebird*, by Igor Stravinsky

Through movement, ballet can express feelings that would be difficult or impossible to say in words. Some ballets are story ballets. Stravinsky's *The Firebird* is one of the finest story ballets of the twentieth century. Based on a Russian folk legend, it tells of Prince Ivan. He discovers a magic garden whose inhabitants are under the spell of an evil king named Kastchei (käs-chā′ē). With the help of the enchanted firebird, Ivan breaks the spell. This releases, among the others, the girl he marries, and all ends happily.

In the Infernal Dance, Stravinsky describes the King Kastchei's evil power through ominous-sounding themes, abrupt changes of instruments and dynamics, and strong rhythms. One can imagine, just by listening to this music, Kastchei's menacing gestures and his domination of the scene, even without seeing his actions on stage.

- Listen to the music and read the description below.

 "Infernal Dance" from *The Firebird,* by Igor Stravinsky

1. Loud chord—brasses and bassoons present ominous theme; theme is repeated.
2. Xylophone joins the proceedings.
3. A flowing melody in the strings.
4. Xylophone alternates with other instruments.
5. Smoother melodic ideas in strings and other instruments, soft and loud.
6. Entire orchestra plays the smoother idea at a loud dynamic level.
7. Suddenly soft, though the scary mood continues.
8. Theme (soft) punctuated by xylophone.
9. Crescendo built with shorter, faster notes.
10. Brasses alternate with other instruments.
11. Faster tempo builds a peak; music ends with one loud chord, then a soft chord.

"Tonight," from *West Side Story*, by Leonard Bernstein and Stephen Sondheim

When *West Side Story* opened on Broadway in 1957, it was quite different from other musical plays of the time. In it, the story of Romeo and Juliet was transplanted to New York's West Side and given a contemporary flavor by the use of popular music styles.

The plot of *West Side Story* concerns two street gangs, the Jets and the Sharks, each of which wants to rule the neighborhood. At the beginning of the story Tony, formerly a member of the Jets, has quit the gang and taken a job in hopes of bettering his life. One night at a dance Tony meets Maria, a Puerto Rican girl. They fall in love. But Maria and Tony's romance is doomed from the start. Maria is the sister of Bernardo, the leader of the Sharks, and is engaged to Bernardo's friend Chino. Despite this the two lovers meet secretly. In a scene reminiscent of the famous balcony scene in *Romeo and Juliet* they sing the beautiful duet "Tonight" on the fire escape outside Maria's apartment.

The two rival gangs plan a rumble (fight) to determine who will rule the neighborhood. Tony tries unsuccessfully to stop the fight and make peace between the two gangs. Bernardo and Tony's best friend Riff fight as everyone else watches. The rules for the fight specify no weapons, but knives are drawn and Bernardo kills Riff. In a grief-stricken rage, Tony takes Riff's knife and kills Bernardo. The gang members scatter as the police arrive.

Anita, Bernardo's girlfriend, learns the outcome of the rumble and goes to Maria to break the news about Bernardo to her. Maria is only concerned about Tony. Angrily, Anita tells her that Tony killed Bernardo. Maria is sorrowful, but is determined to forgive Tony.

Tony and Maria make plans to go away together. When Maria is delayed she sends Anita with a message for Tony. Anita goes to the store where Tony works and encounters some of the Jets. They know she is Bernardo's girlfriend and taunt her. Enraged, Anita gives them a different message for Tony: Chino found out about Tony and Maria, and killed her.

Tony, numb with grief, goes looking for Chino. But Chino finds Tony first, and shoots him in revenge for Bernardo. Maria finds Tony lying in the street. She cradles him in her arms as he dies. United by tragedy, the rival gangs finally make an effort at peace and jointly carry Tony's body away as Maria follows.

West Side Story contains solos, duets, instrumental sections, and ensembles (music in which several people sing at the same time). If several actors were to talk at the same time, the audience would not be able to understand them. However, in music, two or more things can happen at once, and the results will still be understandable. This ensemble, entitled "Tonight," has several different ideas going on at the same time: Maria and Tony express their love for each other; Anita looks forward to an evening of fun; and the opposing gangs plot the rumble that is about to take place.

• Follow the story line in "Tonight" by reading the descriptions.

1. *Jets:* "The Jets are gonna have their day tonight."
   Sharks: "We're gonna hand them a surprise tonight."
   Brief, jazzy introduction, Jets and Sharks in a fast tempo, with a strong rhythmic accompaniment.

2. *Anita:* "Anita's gonna get her kicks tonight."
   Introduced by brief, jazzlike pattern; same melody that was sung by Jets and Sharks, but sung as a solo.

3. *Tony:* "Tonight, tonight."
   A new melody is introduced; rhythmic accompaniment here is more subdued for this soaring, smoother tune, which depicts Tony and Maria's love for each other.

4. *Maria* continues Tony's melody of "Tonight."

5. *Jets:* "The Jets are comin' out on top tonight."
   Strong accompaniment returns, illustrating the warlike mentality of the gangs.

6. *Maria* sings "Tonight" with short comments in the background by the *Jets*, the *Sharks*, *Tony*, and *Anita*. Each melody is different from the others, even though they are all sung at the same time. The quintet reaches an exciting conclusion.

• Decide how the composer provides different music for each character or group.

These scenes are from the film of *West Side Story*. Above, the rumble. Tony (Richard Beymer) is facing forward. Left, Anita (Rita Moreno) and some friends on the roof of their apartment building.

 "Tonight," quintet from *West Side Story,* by Leonard Bernstein and Stephen Sondheim

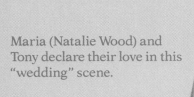

Maria (Natalie Wood) and Tony declare their love in this "wedding" scene.

Lieutenant Kijé Suite, by Sergei Prokofiev

Lieutenant Kijé (kē′ jā) was a Russian film for which Sergei Prokofiev (ser′ gā prō-kō′ fē-ev) composed the score. The story of *Lieutenant Kijé* is a humorous one, set in the nineteenth century. One day the czar of Russia is looking at military reports and misreads the name *Kijé* in an account of a heroic deed. When the czar asks questions about Lieutenant Kijé, his advisors are afraid to tell him that he has made a mistake. Consequently they proceed to make up a life story for the imaginary Lieutenant Kijé.

In the first movement of the suite, "The Birth of Kijé," a solo cornet theme decribes Kijé's birth and some of his supposed military exploits. A separate theme is used to represent Kijé himself. This theme reappears in later movements of the suite whenever Kijé is present.

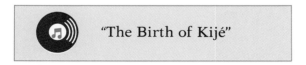

- Listen to the first movement of this suite and identify the instruments that Prokofiev uses to convey the idea of Kijé's military service.

"The Birth of Kijé"

The advisors continue their story, and in the second movement of the suite, "Romance," Kijé falls in love. A "love song" theme is played by string bass, cello, and tenor saxophone. This is followed by themes from Kijé's wedding and the celebration afterward.

A scene from
the 1934 film
Lieutenant Kijé

Prokofiev uses these two themes in the third movement, "The Wedding of Kijé," to describe the relationship between the stately ceremony (Theme 2) and the celebration (Theme 3). Kijé's theme (Theme 1) also is heard throughout.

• Listen and identify which theme you hear for each number.

 "The Wedding of Kijé"

The advisors describe more of Kijé's deeds to the czar. Their plan backfires when the czar is so interested that he asks to meet Kijé! The advisors must do something quickly. They tell the czar that Kijé has died and has been buried with full military honors.

In the fifth and last movement, "The Burial of Kijé," Prokofiev uses many of the themes from the earlier movements to remind the audience of Kijé's life. Then the solo cornet returns with the opening theme as the hero is laid to rest.

"Ev'ry Time I Feel the Spirit," an African American spiritual, arranged by William Dawson

Some musicians **arrange** rather than compose music. In arranging, a musician takes an existing composition and resets it for a different combination of musical resources. For example, a work for two voices may be rearranged for two clarinets.

One of the challenges an arranger faces is not to let the arrangement overpower the unique qualities of the original music. "Ev'ry Time I Feel the Spirit" illustrates William Dawson's sensitive feeling in preserving the characteristics of spirituals in his choral arrangements.

William Dawson, composer, arranger, and conductor

William Dawson, born at the turn of the century, has arranged many African American spirituals. By creating arrangements, he has made it possible for choirs to perform this exciting and expressive music. As choir director at Tuskeegee Institute in Alabama, Dawson has shared his arrangements with people throughout the United States and Europe.

"Ev'ry Time I Feel the Spirit" is one of William Dawson's best-known choral arrangements. He uses strongly syncopated rhythms, contrasts between group and solo singing, and the improvised quality of the choral parts to create an exciting musical setting.

Learn the melody before you listen to a performance of "Ev'ry Time I Feel the Spirit" by the Brazeal Dennard Chorale.

- Perform the melody by singing it or playing it on keyboard or bells.

Ev'ry Time I Feel the Spirit

African American Spiritual

Ev - 'ry time I feel the spi - rit Mov - in' in my heart. I will pray; Yes; ev-'ry

time I feel the spi - rit Mov - in' in my heart. I will pray.

- Listen to the Brazeal Dennard Chorale perform "Ev'ry Time I Feel the Spirit."

 "Ev'ry Time I Feel the Spirit"

The Brazeal Dennard Chorale of Detroit, Michigan, specializes in performing music by African American composers and arrangers. Named after its conductor, the group has performed many concerts in the Detroit area as well as in Michigan and Ohio.

The Brazeal Dennard Chorale. Mr. Dennard is at the lower right.

MUSIC OF THE WORLD'S CULTURES

THE INFLUENCE OF WORLD CULTURES

Musicians, dancers, authors, architects, and sculptors get their ideas from many different sources. They are often influenced by the cultural traditions of other countries.

Sometimes the characteristics of other cultures are obvious. At other times cultural influences may be more difficult to identify. The College Life Insurance headquarters buildings have characteristics of contemporary styles and the styles of ancient Egypt.

- Identify the contemporary characteristics of these buildings.
- Identify the ancient Egyptian characteristics.

Left, the pyramids at Giza, Egypt. Below, the College Life Insurance Headquarters, Indianapolis, Indiana.

Mixing Musical Cultures

In this first section you will listen to music that mixes the characteristics of music of the United States with characteristics of the music of another culture. Some ways musicians do this are to combine instruments, rhythm, melodies, or harmonies of both cultures.

Kogoklaras (kō-gō-klä' räs) is one example of this mix. It combines characteristics of Indonesian music and music of the United States.

Right and below, dancers from the island of Bali, Indonesia. The dancers must practice for years to master these difficult techniques.

- Listen and identify musical characteristics of Indonesia and the United States.

 Kogoklaras, by Vincent McDermott

211

American and Indian Cultures Interact

Other cultures, including that of India, have influenced the music of the United States. Shakti, a musical group from the United States, combines Indian traditional music and instruments with rock style instruments of the United States in "Come On Baby Dance With Me."

- Listen for characteristics of Indian music and music of the United States.

 "Come On Baby Dance With Me," performed by Shakti

You can learn these instrumental parts to perform accompaniments to "Come On Baby Dance With Me."

- Practice each part before performing with the recording.

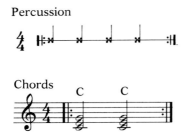

- Form groups. One group should play the percussion part with drumsticks or other percussion instruments. The other group should play the chords on guitar or keyboard.

CHALLENGE Try playing these melodic patterns to "Come On Baby Dance With Me."

212

THE MUSIC OF INDIA

The Hall of Public Audience, Agra, India

"Come On Baby Dance With Me" is a combination of Indian music and music of the United States. Next you will hear Indian concert music. Like Western jazz, Indian concert music is improvised. In some Indian music, one pitch, called a *drone*, is repeated in such a way that it is sounding continuously. This drone pitch provides a background for the creation and performance of rhythmic and melodic patterns. In *Madhu Kauns*, (mä' doo käns), the pitch D-flat (the black key to the left of D on the keyboard) is repeated as the drone.

- Listen for the D-flat drone in *Madhu Kauns*.

 Madhu Kauns

- Play D-flat at the proper time on keyboard or bells as you listen again.

Rhythm patterns in Indian music usually are longer than those in Western music. Instead of two, three, or four beats to a group, Indian rhythm patterns can have ten, twelve, fourteen, or sixteen beats. These patterns are repeated and used as a basis for improvisation.

- Perform the steady beat on percussion instruments with *Madhu Kauns*.
- Next play the D-flat drone and the steady beat with the recording.

CHALLENGE Try playing this rhythm pattern to *Madhu Kauns*.

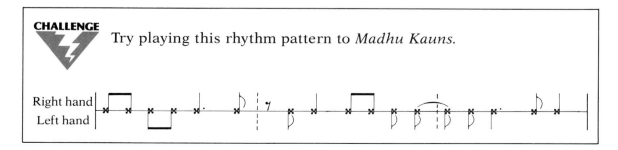

213

Tone Colors in the Music of India

The melody of *Madhu Kauns* is performed on a *sitar* (si' tär). The sitar is a twenty-six-stringed instrument somewhat like a lute. The performer uses six of these strings to play a melody. The rest of the strings vibrate when the melody is played, resulting in a continuous layer of sound.

Top, girls from northern India. Above, Ravi Shankar (center), a world-famous sitar player. The other performers in his ensemble play the tambura (right), a stringed instrument that produces the drone pitches, and the tabla (left), drums.

- Listen again to *Madhu Kauns* and focus on the sound of the sitar.

 Madhu Kauns (excerpt)

The sitar melodies combine with the drone pitch and repeated rhythms played on hand drums to give Indian music its distinctive sound.

The traditional music of India is performed in concert settings. Members of an Indian audience are familiar with the repeated rhythms. As they listen they frequently move their hands silently in time to the rhythm. How is this different from the way an audience in the United States might respond?

214

Xylophone ensembles are popular in many parts of Africa. These performers are members of the Senufo tribe from the Ivory Coast.

MUSIC OF MALI

In the African nation of Mali, *xylophone ensembles* frequently perform complex rhythmic and melodic patterns. Xylophones in an ensemble can vary. Sometimes other instruments perform with the xylophones, for example, guitar, metal clappers, drums, or voice.

Musicians in a xylophone ensemble perform rhythms in several different ways. They can repeat just one rhythm pattern or alternate between patterns. They can echo a pattern that another musician has just played or create new patterns.

- Listen to *Kondawele,* a piece from Mali.

 Kondawele (excerpt)

You can use these rhythms to create a percussion ensemble in the style of those found in Mali.

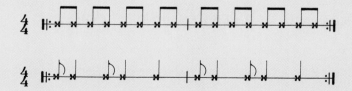

- Perform both lines of rhythm. Use different melodic and percussion instruments for each line.
- Notice how the sound of your ensemble changes when you use different instruments. Try other combinations of instruments.

215

THE MUSIC OF GAMBIA AND THE MUSIC OF ZIMBABWE

The Sounds of Gambia

Rhythmic variety is characteristic of traditional music from the African country of Gambia. *Kelefa ba* (ke-le' fä bä) is an example of this style of music. Each of its rhythm parts is different from the others. When they are performed together, the result is a rhythmically complex and constantly changing musical sound.

• Listen to *Kelefa ba* to hear this rhythmic variety.

Kelefa ba

• Practice each of these rhythm patterns on unpitched percussion instruments.

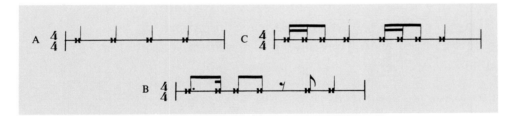

• Compare the rhythm patterns. Which has mostly short note values? Mostly long note values?
• Form three groups. Listen to the changing rhythmic sound as two groups perform two of the rhythm patterns at the same time. Have the third group add the third part.
• Perform the rhythm patterns with the recording of *Kelefa ba*. Listen for the changes in rhythm.
• Practice this melodic pattern on keyboard or bells. Play it with *Kelefa ba*.

• Form four groups to perform the three rhythm patterns and the melodic pattern with *Kelefa ba*.

216

Instrumental and Vocal Sounds of Gambia

Some Gambian music is performed by a solo voice and a stringed instrument called a *kora* (kô′ rä). The kora, a kind of harp-lute, comes in several sizes with from five to twenty-one strings. A small metal disk with metal rings attached produces a rasping sound when the performer plucks or strums the strings.

Throughout West Africa, professional musicians are called *griots* (grē′ ō). In Gambia, griots are very important, because one of their roles is to record the history of the Gambian people. They pass this history on through their music. In contrast, people of Western cultures write books to record their history. The griots compose songs to comment on historical events.

- Listen to *Cedo* (kā′ dō), a Gambian history, to hear the tone color of the kora.

🎵 *Cedo*

Koras are made in many sizes, from small (left) to large (below). *Cedo* is played on a large kora.

The melody in *Cedo* is performed by a singer.

- Listen to *Cedo* again. Identify which of these words best describe the quality of the voice: light or heavy; rough or smooth; strong or weak.

♪ *Cedo*

In this Ivory Coast village, boys of the Yaou tribe listen as a storyteller recounts a tribal legend.

Instrumental and Vocal Sounds of Zimbabwe

Zimbabwe, an African country, is about thirty-five hundred miles southwest of Gambia. The two countries have many cultural differences. However, in their music, the use of voice is similar.

- Listen to *Chemutengure* (che-moo-ten-goo′ re) and identify which of these words best describe the quality of the voice: light or heavy; rough or smooth; strong or weak.

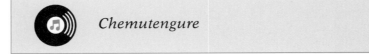

♪ *Chemutengure*

Although the voice is used similarly in the music of Zimbabwe and Gambia, the music of these two countries differs in other ways. For example, Gambian music uses stringed instruments, while in Zimbabwe the *mbira* (m′ bē′ rä) is very important.

The mbira is a melodic instrument. It has a wooden frame with metal tongs attached. The performer plays the mbira by pulling down or plucking each tong, causing it to vibrate. A dried gourd serves to amplify the sound, much like the body of a guitar. In other African cultures, the mbira is called the *sansa, likembe, budongo,* or *kalimba.*

In Zimbabwe, the mbira is used in many different musical ways. It can be used as a solo instrument to express personal feelings. Frequently it is used in religious settings. At other times it accompanies songs of love or politics.

Chemutengure is a composition for the mbira and the voice. Both perform the same melody but at different times.

The mbira is found in many African cultures. Recently, it has become popular in Western musical styles.

- Listen to *Chemutengure* again and follow the melody.

- Practice this accompaniment to *Chemutengure,* then play it with the recording.

The mbira also has been used in American music. Both jazz and popular music groups have included its traditional sounds. Some performers have even used an electrified version.

THE MUSIC OF TURKEY

The *ney* (nā) is a flutelike wind instrument used in the music of Turkey and other countries of the Middle East. It is a hollow cane tube with six finger holes in front and one in back. Unlike the flute, which is held horizontally, the ney is held at an angle when it is played.

The classical music of Turkey is performed on the ney. In this music the performer frequently performs long solos. Sometimes a ney performance includes drums and stringed instruments. The ney is associated with a religious sect, and is played during certain religious services.

The ney is popular throughout the Middle East.

- Play this Turkish scale on keyboard, recorder, or bells. (B-sharp and C are the same key on a keyboard.)

- Listen to *Taksim* (tāk′ sim), or improvisation, *in Mode Segah*. It is performed on the ney. This piece is based on the scale you just played, which is called mode *segah* (sā′ gä).

 Taksim in Mode Segah

220

The ney performer plays along melodic lines that are frequently improvised, or made up on the spot. Single tones of the scale are used as centers around which melodies are developed. In this example, each white note is the center of a melody, or tonal center.

Many times a performer uses *ornaments* with a melody. **Ornaments** are added notes that decorate a basic melody.

- Listen to *Taksim in Mode Segah* again. Try to hear each melodic line and its tonal center. Notice the ornaments the performer adds to the melody, and the long pauses.

Turkey has long been a meeting place between Europe and Asia. These ruins of a fortification are on the Mediterranean coast at Üçagiz near Kale.

THE MUSIC OF JAPAN

In Japan the *nagauta* (nä′ gä-ōō-tä) ensemble is used to accompany a popular form of operalike drama called *kabuki* (kä′ bōō-kē). The nagauta ensemble is similar to the xylophone ensemble of Mali in that it contains percussion instruments as well as pitched instruments. However, the nagauta ensemble performs only in very formal concert settings to accompany the kabuki plays.

The nagauta ensemble contains three different drums: the *o-tsuzumi* (ō′ tsōō-zōō-mē), the *ko-tsuzumi* (kō′ tsōō-zōō-mē), and the *taiko* (tī′ kō). The o-tsuzumi and ko-tsuzumi are doubleheaded laced drums. The player holds the drum on the shoulder and plays it with the other hand. The performer can make the pitch of the ko-tsuzumi high or lower by squeezing the laces while striking the head of the drum. The taiko also is double headed and laced, but is hung from a frame and played with sticks.

The nagauta ensemble also includes two pitched instruments. One is a stringed instrument, the *shamisen* (shä′ mē-sen), and the other, the *bue* (bōō′ ā), is a wind instrument.

Above, the nagauta To-On-Kai in performance. In the front row are one bue, three o-tsuzumi or ko-tsuzumi, and one taiko. The shamisen players in the upper row are awaiting their turn.

- Listen to *Sambaso* (säm′ bä-sō). Follow the description of the music.

 Sambaso

1. Ko-tsuzumi and taiko are heard; voice; drum calls; music becomes faster.
2. Vocal solo; drum calls are heard.
3. The bue is heard, along with the shamisen.
4. The shamisen presents an ascending pattern, then a melodic pattern.
5. Shamisen and bue continue melody; music gradually becomes faster.
6. Bue and drum calls are heard.

Some scenes of Japan. Opposite page, umbrellas drying after painting at a factory. This page, top, a shamisen player. Above, Himeji Castle, near Osaka, the most famous medieval Japanese castle. Left, a festival scene at Sapporo, on Hokkaido island.

THE MUSIC OF INDONESIA

The Sound of the Gamelan

You heard a combination of Indonesian music and the music of the United States in *Kogoklaras* on page 211. This section concentrates on Indonesian sound alone.

The *gamelan* (gä' me-län) is the traditional instrumental ensemble of Indonesia. The ensemble consists of gongs and metallophones, rhythmic drums, flute, and stringed instruments. Some of the gongs play melodies, and others set the meter of the music.

A gamelan from Bali, Indonesia, with gongs, metallophones, and drums. The flute player is near the upper right-hand corner.

In Indonesia, the gamelan accompanies dance, drama, and puppet theatre. Although other types of musical ensembles are common in Indonesia, the gamelan is the most important. There are many different kinds of gamelans, and each kind uses a slightly different set of pitches. Some ensembles perform with five pitches and some use seven. Others use as few as four.

The sound of each instrument in the gamelan has a distinctive quality. As performers repeat rhythmic patterns, the sound joins with others to create layers of sound.

Perform in Gamelan Style

One type of gamelan rhythm develops when the musicians read the same line of rhythm. Instead of performing all of the notes, however, they alternate with other ensemble members to share the notes of the rhythm pattern. The interlocking sounds of their instruments creates an interesting rhythmic and melodic quality.

• Clap this gamelan rhythm.

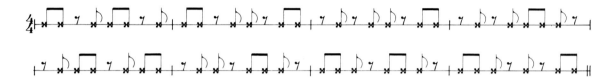

• Perform in gamelan style with a partner:

   1. Each of you should clap or pat every *other* note of the rhythm pattern. Listen closely to the change in the sound of the rhythm as you alternate.
   2. You and your partner should each choose an unpitched percussion instrument.
   3. Perform the rhythm pattern on percussion instruments. Alternate the notes.

   Melodic patterns on pitched instruments also are part of gamelan music. Some patterns are based on a four-pitch scale:

• Perform a two-pitch gamelan-style melodic pattern with a partner:

   1. Each of you should choose one pitch on a bell set, handbell set, xylophone, keyboard, or any pitched object.
   2. With your partner, decide which pitch will be played first.
   3. Perform the rhythm pattern at the top of the page. Alternate with your partner so that you each play every other note. Listen closely to the change in the sounds as you alternate the two pitches.

BORROWING MUSICAL IDEAS

One composer who was deeply influenced by music of another culture was Claude Debussy (klôd də-byu-sē). The aspect of Indonesian music that most interested Debussy was the layering of sound. **Stratification** occurs when layers of melody or sound are heard.

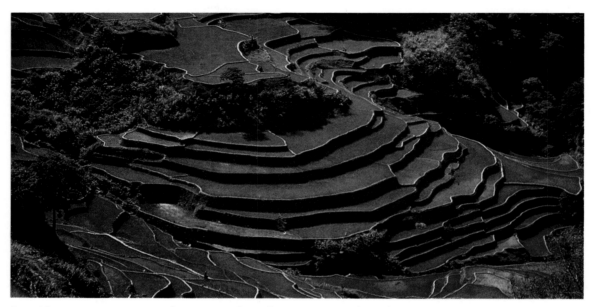

Stratification occurs not only in music but also in nature. These layered rice terraces are on Luzon, in the Philippines.

- Practice this gamelan melody on keyboard or bells.

- Form several groups and perform the melody in stratification. Each group should perform the melody at a different tempo.

The melody you just performed is from *Hudan Mas* (hoō′ dän mäs), a musical work from the island of Java in Indonesia.

- Listen to *Hudan Mas* to hear the layers of sound.

Hudan Mas

CLAUDE DEBUSSY

Claude Debussy (1862–1918) was one of the greatest French composers. Debussy was born in a suburb of Paris and was encouraged to play the piano at an early age. He entered the Paris Conservatory when he was eleven and studied there for eleven years. Debussy created a musical style known as *impressionism*. During his years in Paris he became acquainted with impressionist painters such as Claude Monet, whose works brought out the effects of light and color on nature. He created a style of music that used different harmonies and exotic rhythms to evoke delicate and mysterious moods.

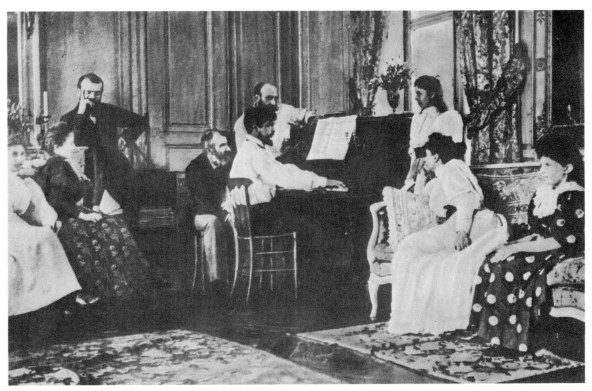

This photo shows the young Debussy playing the piano in a private home in Paris.

Debussy's *"Pagodes"*

At the international Paris Exposition in 1889, Debussy had the opportunity to hear a gamelan ensemble from Java, one of the Indonesian islands. He was fascinated by the sounds of this exotic music. A different gamelan ensemble performed at the 1900 Paris Exposition. Again Debussy was intrigued by the music. The rhythms and melodies he heard challenged Debussy to include some of their characteristics in his own music.

Debussy wrote *"Pagodes"* (pä-gôd′, "pagodas") in 1904, some years after he had heard the gamelan music that influenced this piano composition. Instead of imitating a gamelan ensemble, he included characteristics of gamelan music. He used scales that were not commonly found in Western music. He changed the rhythms of the melodies and added ornamental pitches to them. He also created layers of sound by having more than one melody sounding at the same time.

- Listen to *"Pagodes"* to hear how Debussy was influenced by gamelan music. Read the descriptions.

 "Pagodes," by Claude Debussy

A Section
1. Low gonglike pitches; melody 1; melody 1 with melody 2 below; altered melody 1 with melody 3 below; short melody 4
2. Altered melody 3, using high and low registers; altered melody 1; tempo slows down slightly

B Section
3. Melody 5; melody 1 reappears in part with melody 6 (very loud)
4. Melody 5 (lower); trills

A Section
   Low gonglike pitches; melody 1; melody 1 with melody 2 below; altered melody 1 with melody 3 below; short melody 4
5. Melody 3, using high and low registers; melody 6 (very loud)

Coda
   Melodies 1, 2, and 6, one after the other, with fast, high notes and low, soft gonglike pitches accompanying, to the end

Many peoples of the Far East have built pagodas. Left, below, and bottom, Borobudur Pagoda, on the island of Java, Indonesia

Left, Schwedagon Pagoda, in Rangoon, Burma

LOOKING BACK

See how much you remember.

1. Perform these rhythms from Mali and Indonesia on a percussion instrument with the recording.

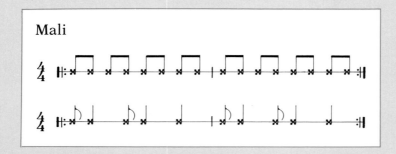

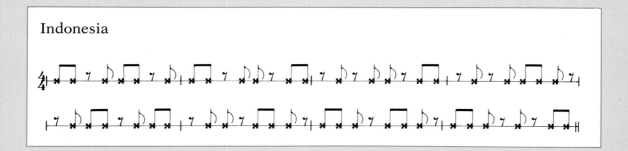

2. Pat the steady beat as you listen to *Madhu Kauns*.

3. Listen and identify the country of origin for each musical example.
   a. Japan or Turkey
   b. India or Mali
   c. Indonesia or Zimbabwe

4. Listen to this excerpt from *Kogoklaras* and identify the two cultures that contributed to this music.

5. Listen and identify the instruments you hear in these excerpts of music from three different cultures.
   a. xylophone ensemble or ney
   b. kora or gamelan
   c. nagauta ensemble or sitar

6. Listen and decide which of these examples contain repetition.

7. Listen to a portion of *Sambaso* and identify the instrument families you hear.

8. Listen to a recording of a gamelan and describe the texture you hear.

9. Listen to a portion of *Cedo* and identify the tone colors in this musical example. Identify the country where you might find this musical style.

KEYBOARDS OF TODAY

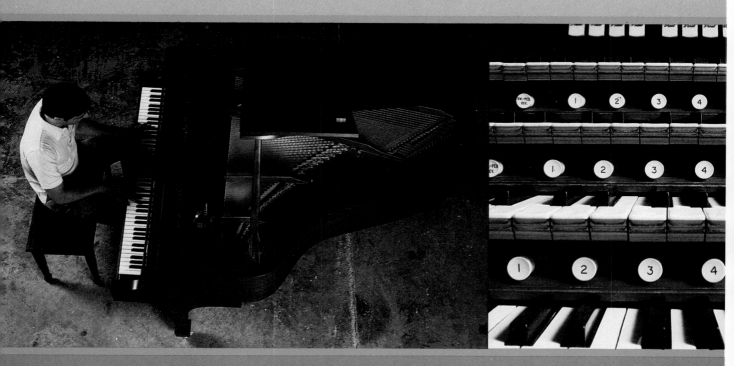

The piano was invented about 1720 and developed into the familiar instrument of today during the first half of the nineteenth century. The pipe organ had its roots in ancient Greece. The electronic organ was invented in the mid-1900s.

Keyboard instruments of today include pianos, organs, and synthesizers, which were developed during the 1960s. Today's synthesizers enable players to produce an almost unlimited variety

Detail from *Harpsichord*, Johann Christoph Weigel

of sounds, even the sounds of other instruments. Through rhythm units (drum machines), sequencers (recording devices), and a variety of tone colors, the synthesizer has become more complex.

Keyboard instruments are used by many popular music groups.

Notice the many sizes and shapes of the keyboards shown here. The arrangement of black and white keys is always the same.

KEYBOARD BASICS

• Listen to these two selections to hear the sounds of different keyboard instruments.

 "Dream of Dreams," by Joe Sample

 "Harmonic Repetition Montage"

The keyboard has sets of white and black keys. Center yourself in front of the keyboard and find each set of *two* black keys up and down the keyboard. C is always the white key to the left, D is the white key in the middle, and E is the white key to the right of the two black keys. Middle C is the C that is closest to the center of the keyboard.

Each set of *three* black keys is a reference point for finding F, G, A, and B. F is always the white key to the left, G and A are the white keys in the middle, and B is the white key to the right of the three black keys.

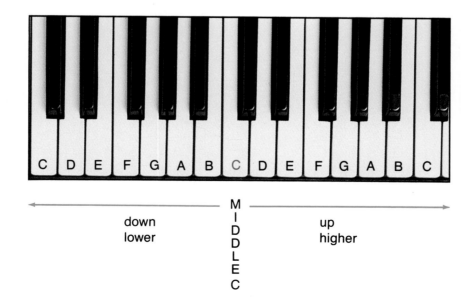

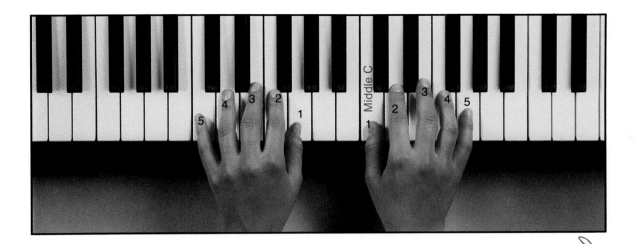

These hands show how the fingers are numbered for the keyboard. Notice that both thumbs are numbered *1*.

You can learn to play chords on the keyboard. A **chord** consists of three or more pitches played together. The twelve-bar blues is a common chord progression, or pattern, used in popular music.

To start you can play one pitch at a time.

- Find pitches C, F, and G on your keyboard. Use the fingers of your right hand as shown.

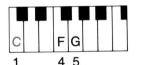

Right hand

- Play the following pitches along with the recording of the twelve-bar blues.

$\frac{4}{4}$ C C C C   C C C C   C C C C   C C C C

     F F F F   F F F F   C C C C   C C C C

     G G G G   F F F F   C C C C   C C C C

 "Twelve-Bar Blues," by Michael Treni

- Play the same pitches again with the twelve-bar blues, this time using the fingers of your left hand as shown.

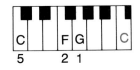

Left hand

235

Learning to Play the C, F, and G Chords

You can play the C chord on the keyboard.

- Start with the left hand and play C with your fifth finger.
  Skip up one white key to the right and use your third finger. You should now be on E with your third finger.
  Skip up another key and use your thumb. You should now be on G with your thumb.
  Play all three notes at the same time.

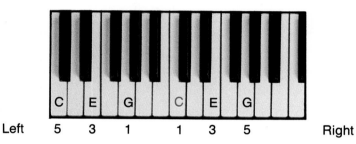

You have just learned to form and play the C chord.

- Now play the C chord with your right hand. Your thumb will be on C, your third finger will be on E, and your fifth finger will be on G.

You can play the F chord.

- Start with your left hand.
  Your fifth finger should be on F.
  Skip up one white key to the right. You should be on A with your third finger.
  Skip up another key and use your thumb. You should be on C with your thumb. Play all three notes together.
- Again, try the chord with your right hand, using your first, third, and fifth fingers.

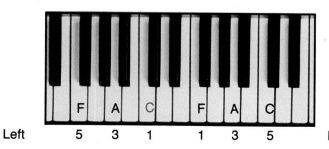

You can play the G chord.

- Start with your left hand.
  Your fifth finger should be on G.
  Skip up one white key to the right. You should be on B with your third finger.
  Skip up another key and use your thumb. You should be on D with your thumb. Play all three notes together.
- Again, try the chord with your right hand, using your first, third, and fifth fingers, the same fingers you used for the C and F chords.

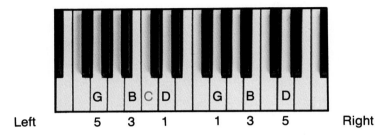

Now that you can play C, F, and G chords with either your left or right hand you can play the twelve-bar blues chord progression.

Many musicians play chords from chord charts. The following chord chart shows the 12 measures or bars of the twelve-bar blues. Three slashes after each chord's letter name indicate that the chord is to be played on every beat of each four-beat measure.

Twelve-Bar Blues

$\frac{4}{4}$ C/// C/// C/// C///
F/// F/// C/// C///
G/// F/// C/// C///

- Play along with the recording of the twelve-bar blues.

 CHALLENGE   Play the twelve-bar blues with both hands.

READING MUSIC AT THE KEYBOARD

The pitches on the keyboard are notated on the **staff** as shown in the following diagram. Pitches can be notated either on lines or in spaces.

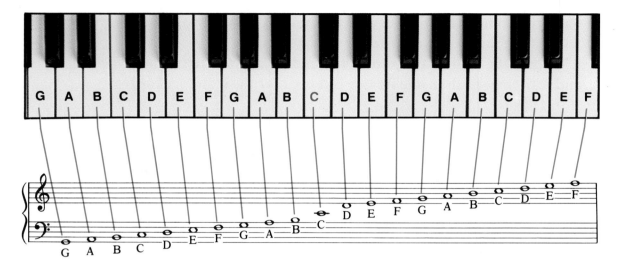

Pitches in the treble clef usually are played with the right hand. Pitches in the bass clef usually are played with the left hand.

Reading Steps

When a melody moves *up or down* on the keyboard from one white key to the next without skipping any notes in between, it is said to move **stepwise**. The steps from one key to the next are notated on the staff as either *line to space* or *space to line*.

- Place the third finger of your left hand on G in the bass clef. Play A, the next note to the right (up), with your second finger. You have moved up a step. Play B, the next note to the right (up), with your thumb. You have moved another step.

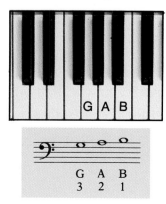

- Read and play these patterns of steps in the bass clef. Say the names of the notes before you play them and again as you play them. Notice the upward and downward motion of each melody.

1.					2.					3.					
F	E	D	E	F	F	G	A	G	F	F	G	A	G	F	E	F
1	2	3	2	1	3	2	1	2	3	3	2	1	2	3	4	3

- Place the thumb (finger 1) of your right hand on G in the treble clef. Play A, the next note to the right (up), with your second finger. You have moved up a step. Play B, the next note to the right (up), with your third finger. You have moved up another step.

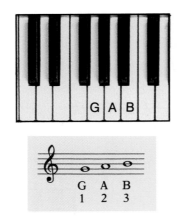

- Read and play these patterns of steps in the treble clef. Say the names of the notes before you play them and again as you play them. Notice the upward and downward motion of each melody.

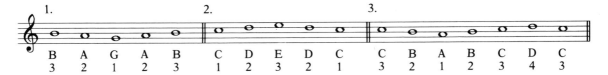

1.					2.					3.					
B	A	G	A	B	C	D	E	D	C	C	B	A	B	C	D	C
3	2	1	2	3	1	2	3	2	1	3	2	1	2	3	4	3

Reading Skips

When a melody moves *up or down* from one note to the next and skips some notes, it is said to move **skipwise**. When you skip one key on the keyboard it is notated on the staff as either *line to line* or *space to space*.

- Play C with the fifth finger of your left hand. Skip a key up to the right and play E with finger 3. Skip another key up to the right and play G with finger 1.

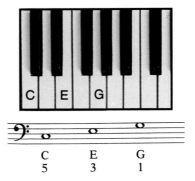

- Read and play these patterns of skips in the bass clef. Say the names of the notes before you play them and again as you play them. Notice the upward and downward motion of each melody.

- Play F with the first finger of your right hand. Skip a key up to the right and play A with finger 3. Skip another key up to the right and play C with finger 5.

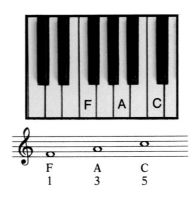

- Read and play these patterns of skips in the treble clef. Say the names of the notes before you play them and again as you play them. Notice the upward and downward motion of each melody.

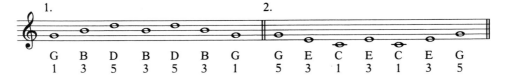

240

THE TWELVE-BAR BLUES

	1	2	3	4 beats
whole note	𝅝			
whole rest	𝄻			
half notes	𝅗𝅥		𝅗𝅥	
half rests	𝄼		𝄼	
quarter notes	𝅘𝅥	𝅘𝅥	𝅘𝅥	𝅘𝅥
quarter rests	𝄽	𝄽	𝄽	𝄽

This chart shows the relationships between notes and rests, or silences, of different durations.

- Read and play this blues progression. Practice each part separately before playing them together.
- Perform this progression with the twelve-bar blues.

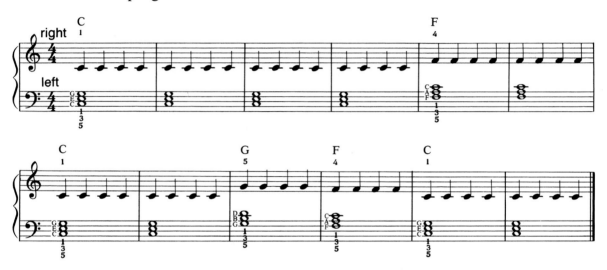

- Play these right hand melodies with the chord sequence. Pattern 1 contains steps. Patterns 2 and 3 contain skips.
- Choose pattern 1, 2, or 3. Play it with the twelve-bar blues. Be sure to play each chord enough times to fit the twelve-bar blues progression.

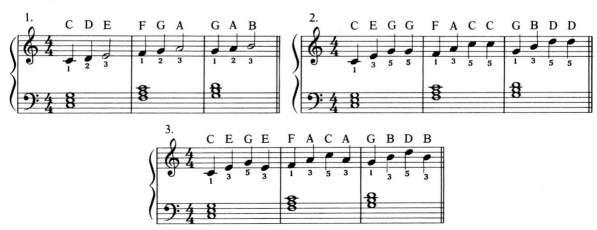

241

You can read and play this blues progression. Note that the chords are in the treble clef, and the melodic patterns are in the bass clef.

- Practice each part separately. Play the chords with your right hand. Play the melody with your left hand. Then play both parts together.
- Perform with the twelve-bar blues.

- Play these left hand melodies with the chord sequence. Pattern 1 measures contain steps and skips. Pattern 2 measures contain steps. Pattern 3 measures contain skips. Notice that when the chord changes to F or G, the beginning note of the left hand melodic pattern changes to F or G.
- Choose pattern 1, 2, or 3. Play it with the twelve-bar blues. Be sure to play each chord enough times to fit the twelve-bar blues progression.

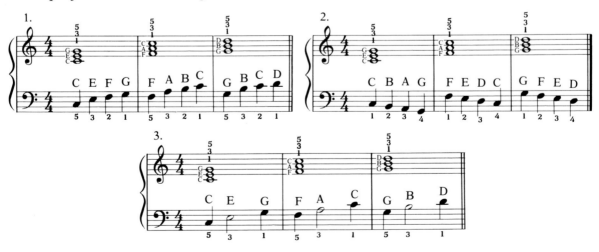

CHALLENGE Create your own melodies by combining right and left hand patterns to play with the twelve-bar blues.

242

TRIADS

The chords you have been playing are based on skips. The three notes are called a **triad**. The bottom note of the chord or triad is called the **root**, the middle note is called the **third**, and the top note is called the **fifth**.

Each measure of melodic pattern 1 below begins on the root, each measure of pattern 2 begins on the third, and each measure of pattern 3 begins on the fifth of each chord.

Two eighth notes ( ) have the same duration as one quarter note ( ).

- Find the starting pitch of each melodic pattern before you play each chord change.

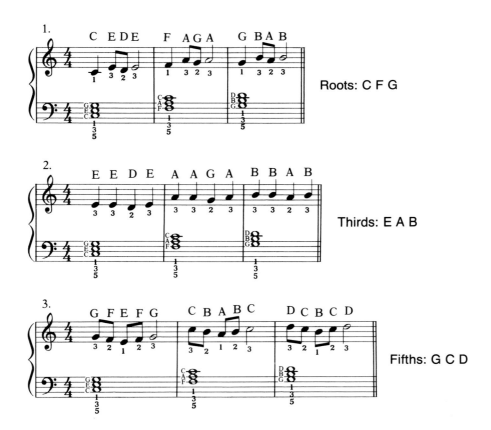

- Play the twelve-bar blues with each pattern.

243

SEVENTH CHORDS

The triads you have been playing contain three pitches. When a chord contains four pitches, the fourth pitch is usually one skip above the fifth. It is the seventh scale tone above the root, called the **seventh**.

- Look at this version of the twelve-bar blues and identify which measures contain chords with four pitches or seventh chords.
- Play the left hand part shown.
  Bb (**B-flat**) is the black key to the *left* of B.

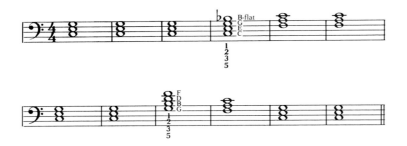

Melodic pattern 1 begins on the root, pattern 2 begins on the third, and pattern 3 begins on the the fifth of each chord. Eb (E-flat) is the black key to the left of E.

- Name the starting pitch of each melodic pattern. Refer to the chart on page 241 if necessary.
- Play each pattern with the twelve-bar blues.

"Several Shades of Blue"

The keyboard selection "Several Shades of Blue" uses the twelve-bar blues progression and several of the melodic patterns you have learned.

- Follow the suggestions in Part I through Part IV to prepare to play "Several Shades of Blue."

Part I: Play the individual notes in each measure all at the same time to form the chord.

Part II: Practice playing fingers 1, 2, and 5 in the right hand on all notes of the chord (Example 1). Later add finger 3 to form a four-note chord (Example 2).

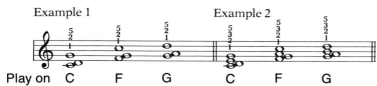

Part III: Practice moving the left hand from the root to the fifth.

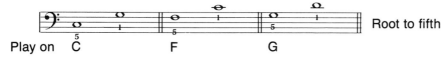

Part IV: Practice with descending quarter notes (Example 1) and then add the root in the right hand (Example 2).

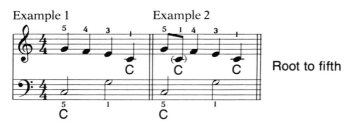

The mark ⎯⎯⎯ stands for **crescendo** (kre-shen' dō), meaning to play gradually louder. The mark ⎯⎯⎯ stands for **decrescendo** (dā' kre-shen-dō), meaning to play gradually softer. The term **simile** (sim' i-lē) means you should continue to follow the marks for crescendo or decrescendo.

Several Shades of Blue

246

- With a group, perform "Several Shades of Blue" by:
    1. playing the root of each chord on guitar, bass, or bells (or synthesizer)
    2. improvising a percussion accompaniment on classroom instruments
    3. playing along with the rhythm section of your keyboard

If you are using a synthesizer with a sequencer, record the root of each chord on your sequencer and replay in repeat mode. Change the keyboard voice on your synthesizer and play along with the sequencer.

A NEW CHORD PATTERN

There are some new chords in this progression. They are shown in both the treble and the bass clef.

- Practice these chords.

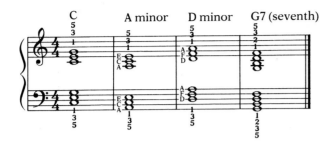

- Find and name the starting pitch of each melodic pattern below before you play it.

In pattern 2, two notes of the same pitch are connected by a curved line called a **tie**. Hold that pitch for the *combined* value of the two notes. In pattern 3, F♯ (F-**sharp**), D♯ (D-sharp), and G♯ (G-sharp) are the black keys to the *right* of F, D, and G, respectively.

- Play this chord progression with each melodic pattern.

Start on the highest pitch of the chord

248

RESHAPING CHORDS

The pitches of a chord can be rearranged to make changes between chords smoother. This is called **revoicing**. It makes transitions from chord to chord sound smoother. It is important to remember that the names of chords do not change when they are revoiced.

- Practice this revoiced chord progression with the left hand.

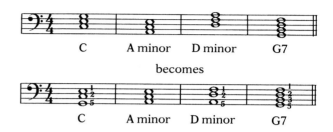

- Create your own melodic pattern in the right hand to play with the left hand chords. Use melodic patterns you have already learned.

- Practice this revoiced chord progression with the right hand.

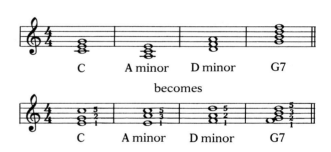

- Create your own melodic pattern in the left hand to play with the right hand chords. Use melodic patterns you have already learned.

"Blue Heart"

"Blue Heart" contains parts of the chord progressions you have learned, along with several of the melodic patterns you have learned. The **fermata** (𝄐) in the last measure tells you to hold those notes slightly longer than usual.

- Practice patterns 1 and 2 before you perform "Blue Heart."

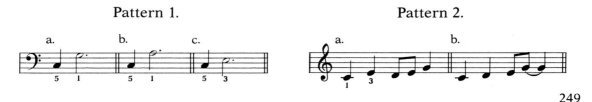

249

Blue Heart

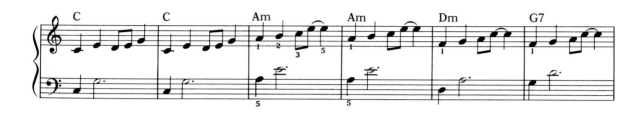

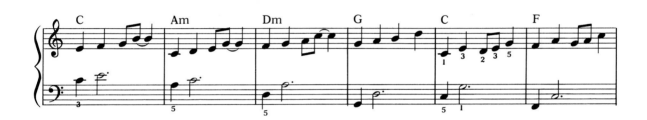

- With a group, perform "Blue Heart" by:
  1. playing the root of each chord on guitar, bass, or bells (or synthesizer)
  2. improvising a percussion accompaniment on classroom instruments
  3. playing along with the rhythm section of your keyboard

If you are using a synthesizer with a sequencer, record the root of each chord on your sequencer and replay in repeat mode. Change the keyboard voice on your synthesizer and play along with the sequencer.

ANOTHER FAMILIAR CHORD PROGRESSION

This chord progression uses chords from the twelve-bar blues. It is
frequently found in popular music.

- Practice the chord changes before you play this progression.

- Practice the left hand melodic patterns below. Find the starting
pitch of each measure before you play it.

Fine (End)

Da Capo al Fine
(Go back to the beginning and play to Fine)

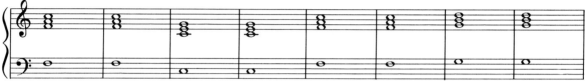

The **natural** sign (♮) cancels a previous sharp or flat in the same
measure.

 CHALLENGE Reverse the parts so that the right hand plays the melodic patterns
while the left hand plays the chords.

"Mama Don't 'Low"

You can play the American folk song "Mama Don't 'Low" as a solo or
with other keyboard instruments or guitars.

● Sing the song first to become familiar with it.

Mama Don't 'Low

American folk song
(arr. P.W.)

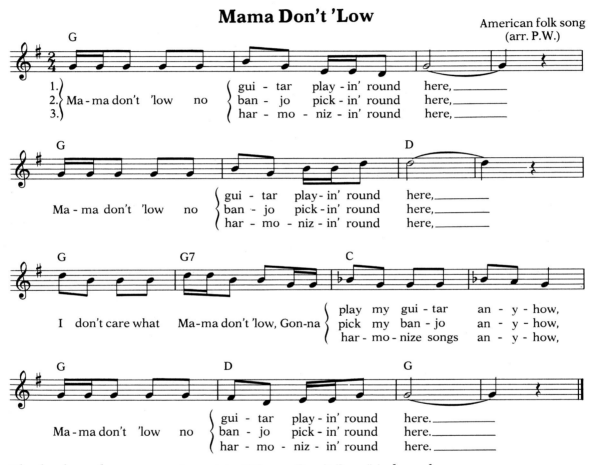

The keyboard accompaniment to "Mama Don't 'Low" is based on
chords G major and C major, which you have learned, and new
chord D major.

● Practice these patterns before you perform "Mama Don't 'Low."

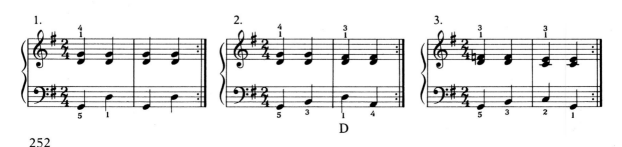

Notice that the music has a new meter signature: $\frac{2}{4}$. In $\frac{2}{4}$ meter, the the quarter note has the steady beat, with two beats in each measure.

- Pat the steady beat and clap the eighth notes to prepare for playing "Mama Don't 'Low."

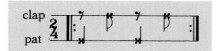

Keyboard Accompaniment to "Mama Don't 'Low"

You can also play this accompaniment with the version for guitar on page 263.

- With a group, perform "Mama Don't 'Low" by:
  1. playing the root of each chord on guitar, bass, or bells (or synthesizer)
  2. improvising a percussion accompaniment on classroom instruments
  3. playing along with the rhythm section of your keyboard

If you are using a synthesizer with a sequencer, record the root of each chord on your sequencer and replay in repeat mode. Change the keyboard voice on your synthesizer and play along with the sequencer.

253

PLAYING THE GUITAR

- Listen to these compositions for guitar. How do they sound alike? How do they sound different?

 Concerto in D Major for Guitar and Orchestra, Third Movement, by Antonio Vivaldi

Detail from *Presentation in the Temple*, Vittore Carpaccio, ACCADEMIA, Venice

 "Hickory Hollow," performed by Banks and Shane

PARTS OF THE GUITAR

In this section you will learn to play strum patterns, chords, and bass parts on the guitar. The four lowest strings of the six-stringed guitar can be tuned to the same pitches as the four strings of the electric bass. You can play bass parts on either instrument.

tuning machines

frets

nut

neck

fingerboard

strings

sound hole

body

bridge

tuning machines

nut

neck

frets

fingerboard

body

bridge

pickup

controls

256

TUNING YOUR GUITAR

The tuning most often used for guitar and bass is pictured here as it relates to the keyboard. The four strings of the electric bass are tuned to the same pitches (one octave below) as the four lowest strings on a six-stringed guitar.

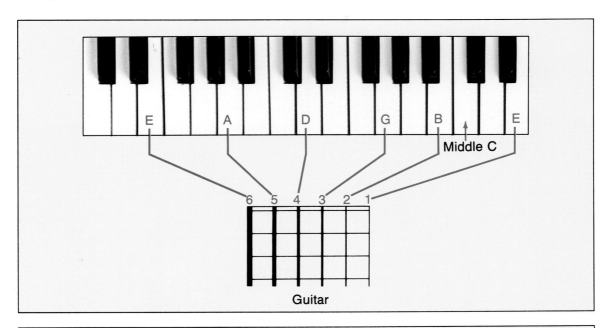

Guitar

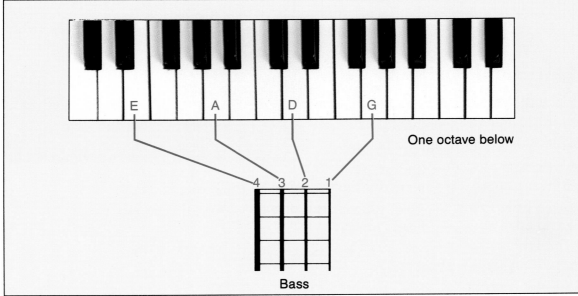

Bass

You can use two alternate tunings for some of the songs in this section. You will find these tunings, as well as chord frames for the songs, on pages 276–277.

257

HOLDING THE GUITAR OR ELECTRIC BASS

Left-Hand Position

Place the pad of your left thumb
in the center back of the guitar
neck. Curve your fingers over the
strings, keeping your palm away
from the neck. The fingers are numbered from the index finger (1)
to the little finger (4). Your fingers **fret**, or press down, the strings
for single notes or to form chords.

Right-Hand Position

Curve the fingers and **strum**, or brush down across the strings with
your fingernails. A down strum is indicated by this sign ⊓.

Brush up across the strings with your thumbnail for an up
strum (⋁).

Strum Patterns for Guitar

Practice these rhythm patterns on **open** (unfretted) strings, or with any chords you already know. Play the downward (⌐) and upward (∨) strums where indicated.

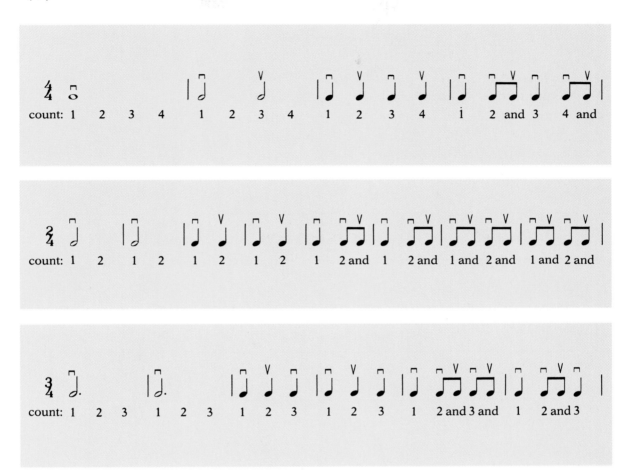

READING A BASS PART IN TABLATURE

Bass parts for either the six-stringed guitar or the electric bass can be written in *tablature*. **Tablature** is a picture of the guitar strings divided into measures of music.

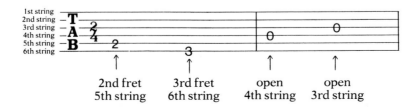

The six lines represent the six strings of the guitar. The numbers on the line indicate the frets. An *O* indicates an open, or unfretted, string. In some tablature the rhythms are shown above the fret numbers. Here the rhythm is ♩ ♩ | ♩ .

More commonly, tablature symbols are used. They are shown with their equivalents in staff notation. The fret number is written inside the note head. The fret number replaces the note head for dotted quarter notes, quarter notes and eighth notes. The rests are the same as in staff notation.

NAMES	STAFF NOTATION	TABLATURE SYMBOLS
whole note	𝅝	2 (just the number)
dotted half notes	𝅗𝅥. 𝄐·	②. ②·
half notes	𝅗𝅥 𝄐	② ②
dotted quarter notes	♩. 𝄑·	2. 2·
quarter notes	♩ 𝄑	2 2
eighth notes	♪ 𝄾	2♪ 2
eighth notes	♫ ♫	2 2 2 2

This is how the symbols look in tablature.

Unless otherwise indicated, the left hand fingering is the same number as the fret.

260

PLAYING CHORDS

A chord diagram or frame shows where to place your left fingers on the fingerboard to fret, or form, a chord. The number in the circle indicates which finger to use. The circle shows you where your finger belongs. An *X* means that a string is not played.

- Practice the E minor and D major chords and the accompaniment patterns for "Drunken Sailor." Then play them with the song.

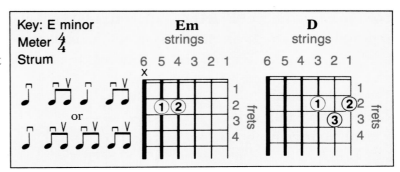

Drunken Sailor

Traditional

Em

What shall we do with a drunk-en sail-or, What shall we do with a drunk-en sail-or,

Em   D   Em

What shall we do with a drunk-en sail-or, Ear-lye in the morn-ing?

Refrain   Way, hey, and up she rises, (*3 times*)
          Earlye in the morning.
     2.   Throw him in the longboat till he's sober, (*3 times*)
          Earlye in the morning.
     3.   Pull out the plug and wet him all over, (*3 times*)
          Earlye in the morning.

ADD A BASS PART

You can play a bass part for this song on the four lowest strings of a six-stringed guitar or on the electric bass. The top line shows the part in staff notation.

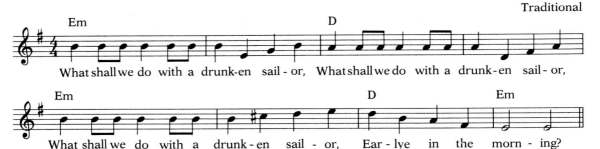

Staff Notation

Tablature for Bass

261

BASS PATTERNS

Bass patterns involve playing the lowest notes of a chord separately from the other notes. In "Mama Don't 'Low," the chords are G major, G7, D7, and C major.

To play a bass pattern, first fret the chord. Then pluck *only* the single bass note shown in the tablature. Follow that with a downward strum on the rest of the strings for that chord. Then repeat the pattern. Note that the symbol ⸮ means the strum should be the same duration as an eighth note. For the G major chord:

1. Fret the chord
2. Pluck *only* this string with your right thumb

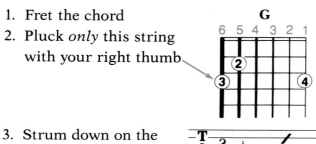

The left hand fingering for G and G7 chords is *not* the same as the fret number. The left hand fingering is shown in parentheses above the tablature.

3. Strum down on the remaining strings

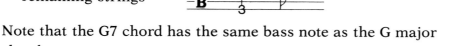

Note that the G7 chord has the same bass note as the G major chord.

- Fret the D7 chord, pluck the fourth string bass note, and strum all the strings *except* the sixth string.

- Fret the C major chord, pluck the fifth string bass note, and strum all the strings except the sixth.

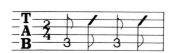

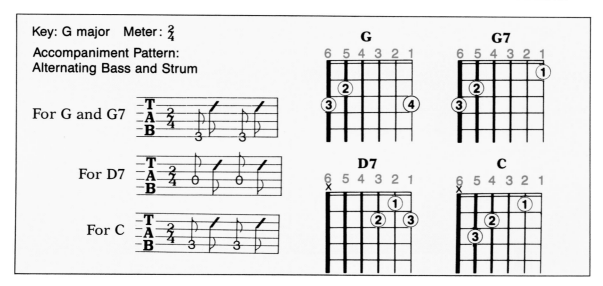

262

Mama Don't 'Low

American folk song (arr. P.W.)

BASS RUNS

A **run** is a stepwise pattern of notes that connects two chords in a song. Runs can be played on the six-stringed guitar. Each note in a run is played individually, usually in an even rhythm. The symbol ⌐ means the strum should be the same duration as a quarter note.

To play Bass Run 1:
1. Fret and play the bass note and the chord in the previous measure.
2. With your right thumb, pluck the single notes shown in the tablature. Change the left hand fingers as necessary.
3. Fret and play the next bass note and chord.

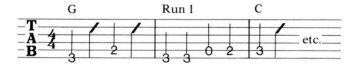

Play Bass Run 2 in the same way:

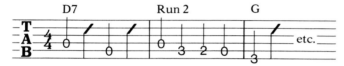

- Practice these runs until they sound smooth, then play them where they are indicated in "The Wabash Cannonball."

Notice that in this song, the bass notes for each chord alternate.

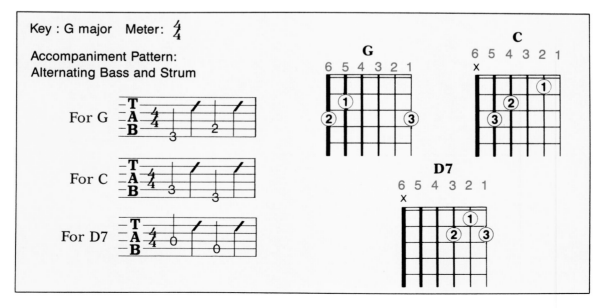

The Wabash Cannonball

Traditional

From the great At-lan-tic O-cean to the wild Pa-ci-fic
Refrain Now— lis-ten to the jin-gle, the— rum-ble and the

shore, From the coast of Cal-i-for-nia to ic-y Lab-ra-
roar As she glides a-long the wood-lands, through the hills and by the

-dor. She's long and tall and hand-some, she's known to one and
shore. Hear the might-y rush of en-gine, hear the lone-some ho-boes

all, that heav'n-ly com-bin-a-tion, the Wa-bash Can-non-ball.
call As they trav-el a-cross the coun-try on the Wa-bash Can-non-ball.

265

THE SLIDE

A **slide** is a kind of slur in which you fret two different pitches but pluck the string only once. The bass part in this song has a slide, on the sixth string. To play a slide:

1. Fret the string with the left hand finger indicated.
2. Pluck that string with your right thumb.
3. *At the same time,* slide the left hand finger up or down to the second fret number indicated. You will hear the pitch move up or down, too.

For example, to play , start on the second fret and slide to the third fret.

In this bass part for "The Wreck of the Edmund Fitzgerald," most of the left hand fingerings are *not* the same as the fret numbers. The left hand fingerings are shown in parentheses above the tablature.

This song is in a new meter, ¾, with *three* beats to a measure.

The song contains one new chord: A minor.

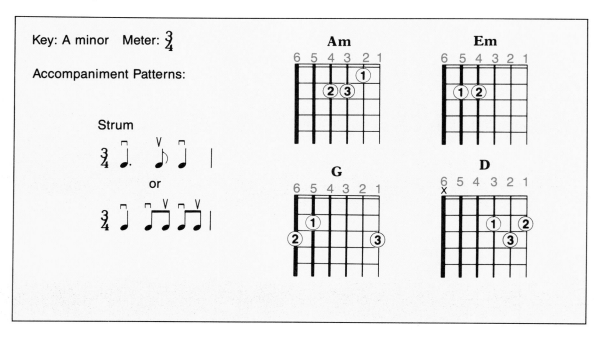

* Play "The Wreck of the Edmund Fitzgerald" with the bass part. Then play it again with the chord accompaniment.

The Wreck of the Edmund Fitzgerald

Words and music by Gordon Lightfoot

You will find the rest of the verses to this song on page 132.

PLAYING THE BLUES

One basic rhythm pattern for the blues is

count: 1   2   3   4

- Play it with a relaxed swing of long and short sounds.

- Practice this rhythm with the G, C, and D chords.
  You can play an accompaniment to "Worried Man Blues" using the rhythm pattern shown above.

The Blues Shuffle

The **blues shuffle** pattern combines the rhythm you have learned with two alternating chords, a root chord, and the same chord with an added tone, called the sixth.

root chord   **G**   root chord   **G 6**
          6 5 4 3 2 1 with added 6 5 4 3 2 1 added sixth
                    sixth

Play the root chord (G, C, or D) on the first and third beats of the measure. Play the sixth chord (G6, C6, or D6) on the second and fourth beats of the measure. You need to move only one finger back and forth to make the change from one chord to the other.

- Play the blues shuffle with these chords from "Worried Man Blues."

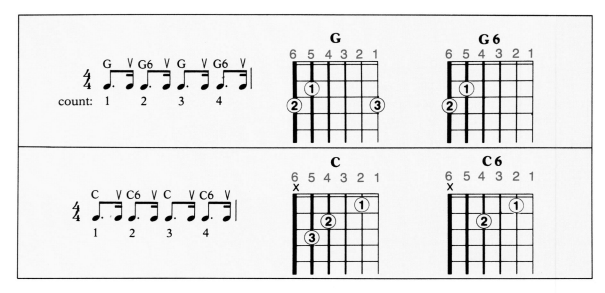

268

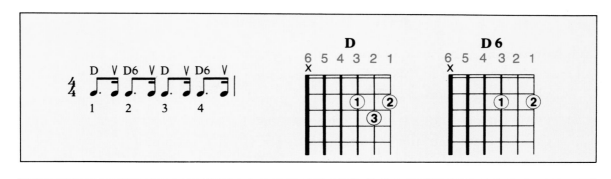

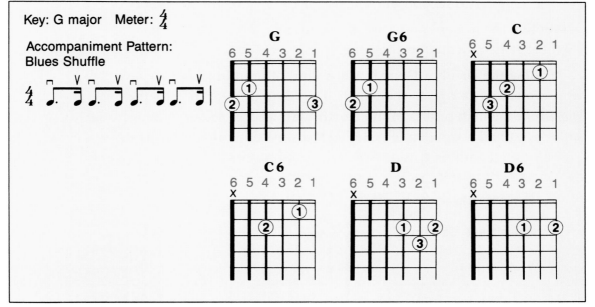

Worried Man Blues

Traditional

THE HAMMER-ON

In a **hammer-on**, you pluck an open string, then fret it, to play two pitches. The bass part to this song includes a hammer-on.

To play this hammer-on:

1. Pluck the open fourth string with your right thumb.
2. *Quickly* fret ("hammer") the second finger of your left hand onto the second fret of the fourth string. You will hear two pitches. The second pitch lasts for the rest of the measure.

• Practice the hammer-on until it sounds smooth, then play it where it is indicated in the song.

"Follow the Drinkin' Gourd" was a kind of map in song for slaves who wanted to escape to the North. The "Drinkin' Gourd" was the Big Dipper, which points to the North Star. The "old man" was a sailor who had a wooden leg. He led the way along the riverbank.

The song contains two new chords: B minor and A.

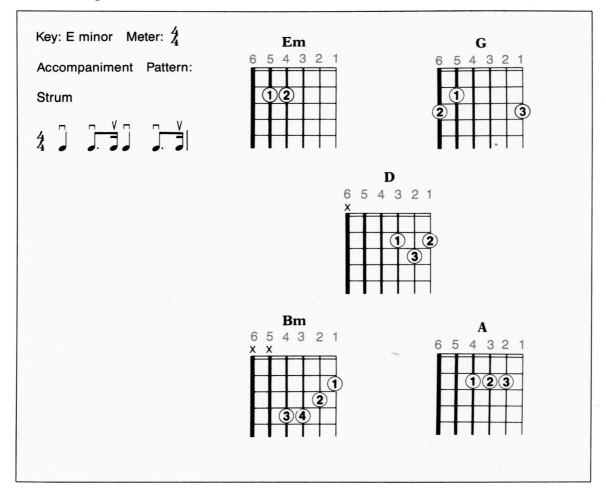

Follow the Drinkin' Gourd

Traditional

Verse 1. When the sun comes back and the first quail calls,____
2. Now the riv-er bank-'ll make__ a might-y good road;____ The
3. Now the riv - er ends____ be - tween two hills;_____

Fol - low____ the Drink-in' Gourd.__Then the Old Man is a-wait-in' for to
dead trees____ will show you the way. And the left__ foot,_ peg - foot,__
Fol - low____ the Drink-in' Gourd.__ And__ there's an-oth-er riv - er on the

car - ry you to free-dom, Fol - low the Drink - in' Gourd.
trav - el - in'____ on, ____ Fol - low the Drink - in' Gourd.
oth - er____ side, ____ Fol - low the Drink - in' Gourd.

Refrain Fol - low_____ the Drink - in' Gourd,_ Fol - low_____ the

Drink - in' Gourd,_ For the Old Man is a - wait - in' for to

car - ry you to free-dom, Fol - low the Drink - in' Gourd.

SETTING THE MOOD OF A SONG

Try to catch the mood of "The Ghost Ship" as you play the guitar
part or the bass part. This song has one new chord: B7.

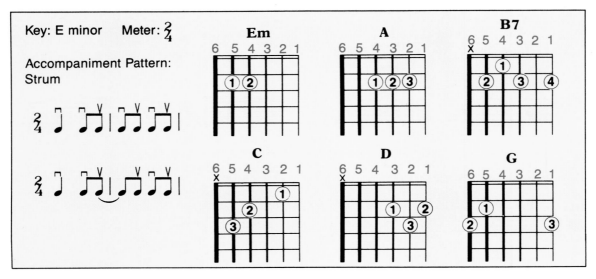

The Ghost Ship

Words and music by
Don Besig and Nancy Price

watch all a-lone that night when I heard a wail-ing cry._____ As I

strained to see what the sound could be, some-thing flashed and caught my eye._____

Refrain
_____ And the cold wind blew,_____

_____ and the cold wind blew._____

2. 'Twas then I spied off the starboard side a strange, mysterious sight.
   I froze with fear as it drifted near like a ghost in the dark of night.
   I could see a sail on a broken mast and deserted decks below.
   From all around came a mournful sound, but I saw not a living soul!

3. Well, I held fast to the forward mast as the ship moved slowly on.
   And I watched that way 'til the break of day, when I knew that it fin'lly
     had gone.
   Oh, they laughed and joked as I told my tale to the captain and the men.
   But the story's true, I can promise you, and it's sure to happen again.

AN ARPEGGIO ACCOMPANIMENT

An **arpeggio** is a chord whose notes are played one at a time, rather than all at once.

To play an arpeggio:

1. Fret the chord.
2. Pluck the strings indicated, one at a time and in rhythm, with your right hand fingers. Finger numbers for the right hand are shown in parentheses *below* the arpeggio. They are the same as for the left hand.

- Practice these arpeggios. Notice that the bass note changes from the fourth to the fifth to the sixth string. The upper strings remain the same for all the chords.

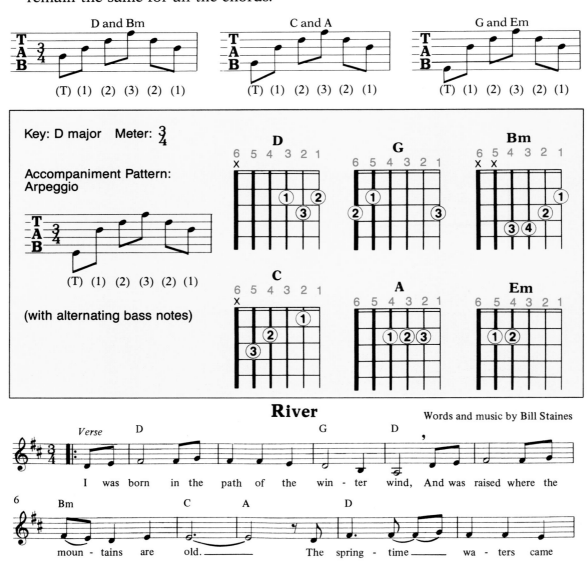

River

Words and music by Bill Staines

Verse

I was born in the path of the win - ter wind, And was raised where the moun - tains are old. _____ The spring - time _____ wa - ters came

2. I've been to the city and back again;
   I've been touched by some things that I've learned,
   Met a lot of good people, and I've called them friends,
   Felt the change when the seasons turned.
   I've heard all the songs that the children sing
   And I've listened to love's melodies;
   I've felt my own music within me rise
   Like the wind in the autumn trees.

   Refrain

3. Someday when the flowers are blooming still,
   Someday when the grass is still green,
   My rolling waters will round the bend
   And flow into the open sea.
   So here's to the rainbow that's followed me here,
   And here's to the friends that I know,
   And here's to the song that's within me now;
   I will sing it where'er I go.

   Refrain

ALTERNATE TUNING: D MAJOR

You can use this tuning to play "The Wabash Cannonball" and "Worried Man Blues."

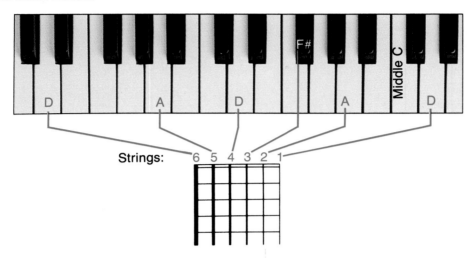

"The Wabash Cannonball"

To play the alternating bass and strum with your right hand, pluck the sixth string with your right thumb for all three chords, then strum the rest of the strings. Omit the bass runs in this tuning. G and C are bar chords. To fret a bar chord, press your index finger down firmly across *all* the strings on fret indicated.

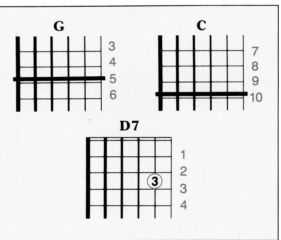

"Worried Man Blues"

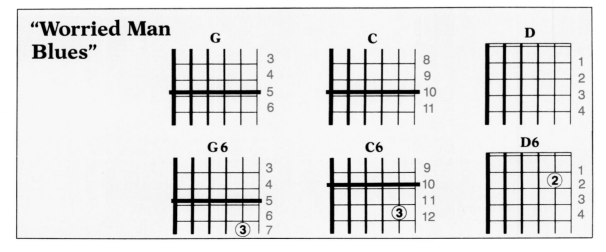

ALTERNATE TUNING: D MINOR

You can use this tuning to play "Drunken Sailor" and "The Wreck of the Edmund Fitzgerald."

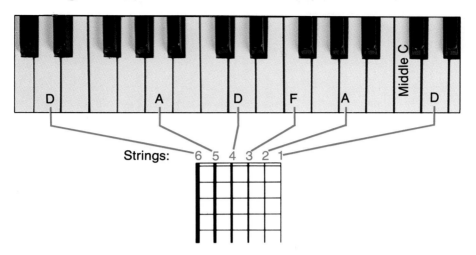

"Drunken Sailor"

E minor is a bar chord (as are A minor and G major below). To fret a bar chord, press your index finger down firmly across all the strings on the fret indicated.

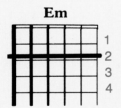

"The Wreck of the Edmund Fitzgerald"

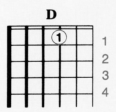

CHORAL SINGING

Detail from *Cantoria*, Luca della Robbia, MUSEO DEL OPERA DEL DUOMO, Florence

CHECKING YOUR VOICE RANGE

Every person's voice has its own unique sound. However, the pitch range in which you sing falls into a group or category. These categories are: **soprano, alto, tenor,** and **baritone.**

This chart shows the approximate singing ranges for young adult singers.

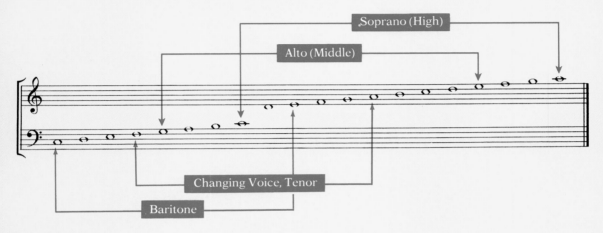

- Sing "America" in this key.

America

Words by Samuel F. Smith
Music by Henry Carey

My coun - try 'tis of thee, Sweet land of lib – er - ty,

Of thee I sing; Land where my fa - thers died, Land of the

pil – grim's pride, From ev - 'ry___ moun - tain-side Let__ free-dom ring.

If you can sing the upper octave more comfortably you probably are either a **soprano** or an **alto.**

If you can sing the lower octave more comfortably you are probably either a **changing voice,** a **tenor,** or a **baritone.**

- Sing "America" in this key.

If you can sing the B section in the upper octave more comfortably you are probably a **soprano.**

If you can sing the B section in the lower octave more comfortably you are probably an **alto.**

- Sing "America" in this key.

If you can sing the A section in the upper octave more comfortably you are probably a **changing voice** or a **tenor.**

If you can sing the A section in the lower octave more comfortably you are probably a **baritone.**

HOW TO PRODUCE A GOOD CHORAL SOUND

To **breathe** properly for singing, you must maintain good posture. Good **posture** means sitting or standing up straight, placing the feet flat on the floor, and holding the chest high so you have enough airflow to support the phrase you're singing. It's easy—try it.

Proper **placement** of tone means maintaining a sameness in the quality of sound throughout your vocal range. Proper placement is not achieved quickly. Practice it every time you sing a song.

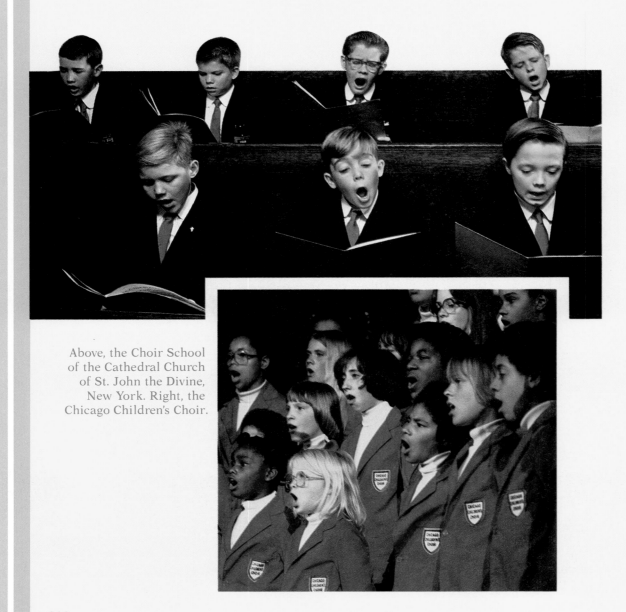

Above, the Choir School of the Cathedral Church of St. John the Divine, New York. Right, the Chicago Children's Choir.

Vowels

Vowel sounds are important in singing because they are the sounds that are sustained, or held. Examine this diagram of **target vowels** and practice shaping each one with your lips to produce the correct sound. Every word in the text of a song will have at least one target vowel on which you can focus.

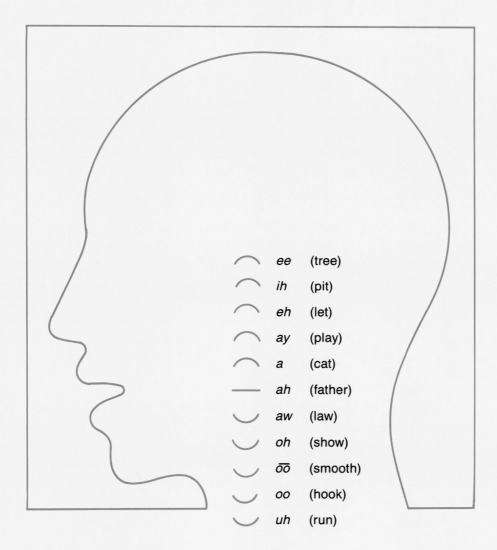

ee (tree)
ih (pit)
eh (let)
ay (play)
a (cat)
ah (father)
aw (law)
oh (show)
o͞o (smooth)
oo (hook)
uh (run)

- Focus on producing clear vowels when you are learning to sing "I'm Goin' Home on a Cloud" on page 284.

This spiritual is a partner song. It presents four different melodies that can be sung at the same time.

- Learn to sing each of the four melodies before performing them together.

I'm Goin' Home on a Cloud

Spiritual
Arranged by Sean Deibler

I. One these fine morn-ings at break of day, I'm go - in' home on a

II. Ev - 'ry morn - ing, ev-'ry day,_ Close my eyes and I be -

III. Spread my wings and fly a - way, Fly up to hea-ven on a

IV. Al – le – lu – ia, Sing to the Lord a song of love and

cloud. King Death goin' find me here at my play,

- gin to pray, Thank the Lord for all His __ ways,

big white cloud. I'm goin' fly _____ high up - on a

joy! Al – le – lu – ia, Sing His name.

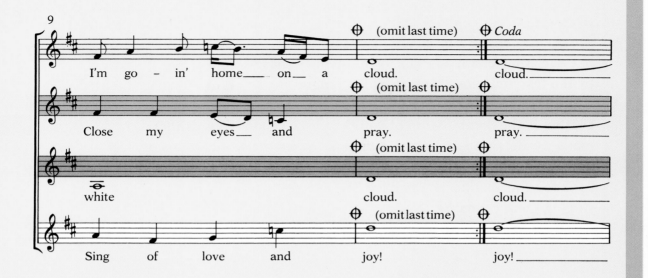

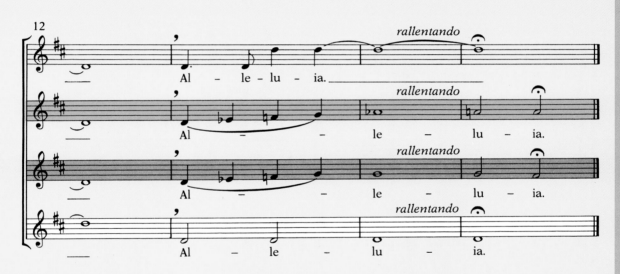

Consonants

- Say each **consonant** sound shown. Identify those sounds shaped by the lips and those shaped by the tongue.

  B V M P   D J T S G C

  Diction is the combination of vowel and consonant sounds that make words. Crisp and precise diction makes the words of a song understandable.

- Look for consonants in "Over the Sea to Skye" and practice singing them correctly.

Over the Sea to Skye

Words by Robert Louis Stevenson
Old Highland rowing song arr. by M.J.

*Tacet (ta' set) means that Part II will not sing until indicated.

BUILDING A CHORAL ENSEMBLE

You have learned that characteristics of good choral singing include:

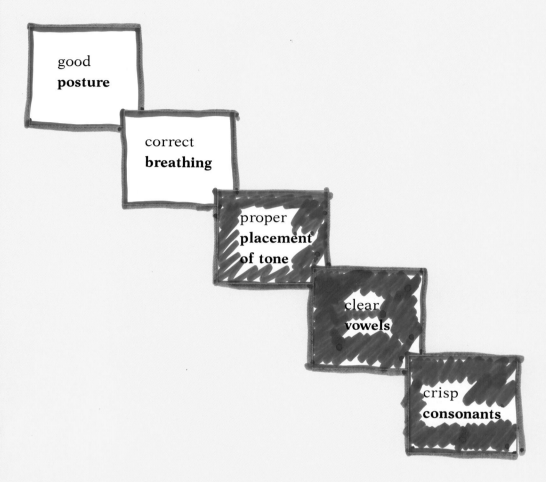

good **posture**

correct **breathing**

proper **placement of tone**

clear **vowels**

crisp **consonants**

To practice these characteristics of good singing, try these warm-ups with "The Rhythm of Life."

Maintain good posture so that you can breathe correctly to sustain and support the airflow. Sing each phrase of the song with the syllable *loo* in place of the words. For proper placement of tone, you should work for maintaining a sameness in the quality of sound throughout the song. Sing the syllable *vee* in place of the words. Then practice the words, working for clear vowels and crisp consonants.

One more characteristic of good choral singing is **blend**. You should blend your voice with those of the other singers to create a unified sound. This way the many individual voices sound like one. Keep this in mind as you sing "The Rhythm of Life" together.

The Rhythm of Life

Words by Dorothy Fields (adapted)
Music by Cy Coleman
Arranged by Richard Barnes, adapted by V.L.

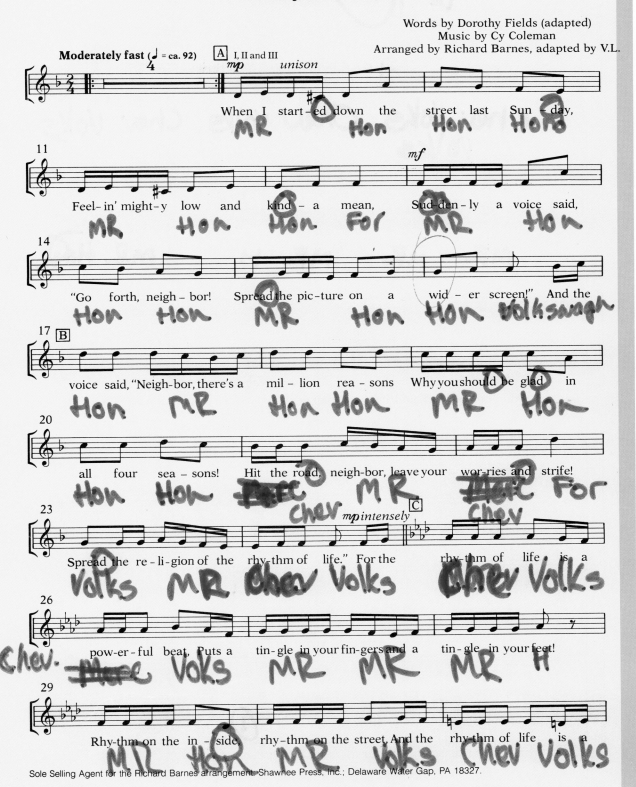

Sole Selling Agent for the Richard Barnes arrangement: Shawnee Press, Inc.; Delaware Water Gap, PA 18327.

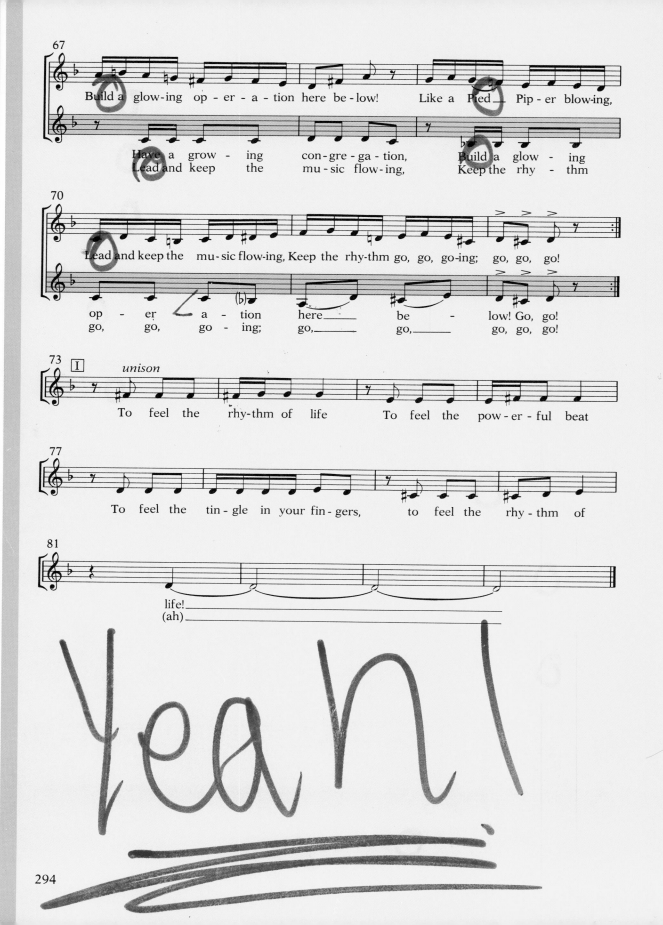

BUILDING MUSIC READING SKILLS

When someone can read music, he or she can look at a line or page of music and mentally hear how it sounds. The following preparations will help you develop your music reading skills.

Use the **tone ladder** to review the pitches of the major scale. Use syllables or numbers.

- See, hear, and sense the intervals between the pitches as you sing up and down the tone ladder.

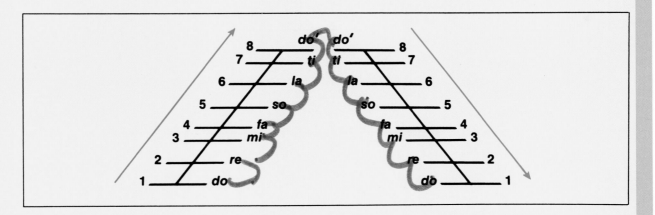

Preparation 1

- Clap this rhythm pattern.

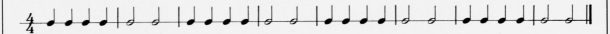

- Add these pitches from the tone ladder to the same rhythm pattern. Sing the pitches with syllables or numbers.

When you sing pitches that are next to each other, for example, 1 to 2 or 3 to 2, the melody is said to move **stepwise.**

- Use the tone ladder to create your own stepwise melody to the same rhythm pattern.

Preparation 2

- Use the tone ladder to help you find the pitches in the beginning of the melody of "April Weather."

Where are the steps between pitches? Where are the **skips,** or spaces, between pitches? Find the repeated pitches.

Preparation 3

Here is the same melody with a second part as it appears in "April Weather."

- Practice each part separately. Then sing both parts together. Find this section in the music.

- Use syllables or numbers to sing this pattern.

In which voice part do you find this pattern?

April Weather

Words by Lizette Woodworth Reese
Music by C. M. Shearer

♩ = c. 128

I

1. & 3. Oh, hush, my heart and take thine ease, For here is A - pril
2. The li - lac bush is sweet a - gain; Down ev - 'ry wind that

II

1. & 3. Oh, hush, my heart and take thine ease, For here is A - pril
2. The li - lac bush is sweet a - gain; Down ev - 'ry wind that

(3rd time to 3rd ending)

wea - ther! The daf - fo - dils be - neath the trees Are all a - row to -
pass - es, Fly flakes from hedge-rows and from lane; The bees are in the

wea - ther! The daf - fo - dils be - neath the trees Are all a - row to -
pass - es, Fly flakes from hedge-rows and from lane; The bees are in the

molto rit. on 2nd verse

- geth - er. The thrush is back with his old note; The scar - let tu - lips
grass - es. And Grief goes out, and Joy comes in, And care is but a

- geth - er.
grass - es.
Thrush is back with his old note; The scar - let
Grief goes out, and Joy comes in, And care is

a tempo on 2nd verse

blow - ing; And white, ah, white as my love's throat The dog - wood boughs are
feath - er; And ev - 'ry lad his love can win, For here is A - pril

tu - lips blow-ing; And white, ah, white as my love's throat The dog-wood boughs are
but a feath - er; And ev - 'ry lad his love can win, For here is A - pril

1 & 2

grow - ing.
weath - er.

3

geth - er.

grow - ing.
weath - er.

geth - er.

297

Phrases in "The Rose" begin with an incomplete measure, called a **pickup.**

Preparation 4

- Clap or tap these three patterns in order. Listen for the differences among the patterns.

- Find the third pattern in the phrase below.
- Form two groups. Sing this phrase in two parts. Notice that the lower part is notated in the bass clef.

Some say love it is a ri - ver that drowns the ten - der reed.

The Rose

Words and music by Amanda McBroom
Arr. by V.L.

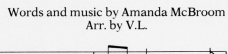

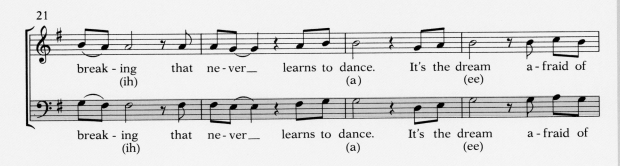

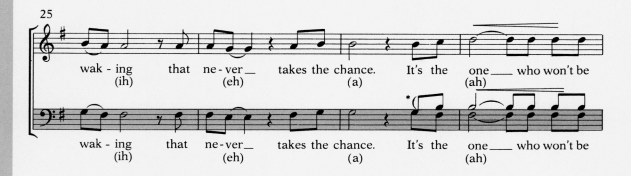

wak - ing that ne - ver___ takes the chance. It's the one___ who won't be
(ih) (eh) (a) (ah)

ta - ken who can not seem to give.___ It's the soul a - fraid of
(eh) (ih) (oh)
unis.

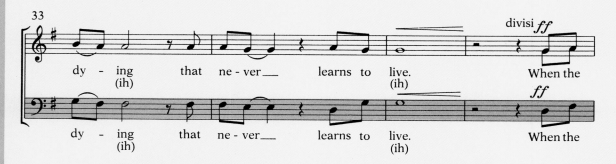

dy - ing that ne - ver___ learns to live. When the
(ih) (ih)

divisi *ff*
ff

night___ has been too lone - ly and the road___ has been too long, And you
(ah) (ee) (oh) (ah)

*Optional divisi

300

think__ that love is on - ly for the luck - y and the strong, Just re -
(ah)

think__ that love is on - ly for the luck - y and the strong,
(ah)

mem-ber__ in the Win-ter__ lies the
(eh)

far be - neath__ the bit-ter snow__ lies the
(ee)

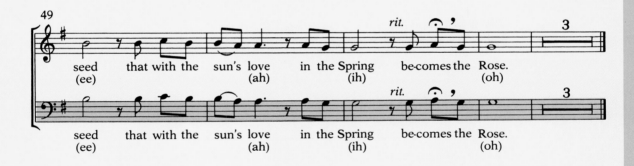

seed that with the sun's love in the Spring be-comes the Rose.
(ee) (ah) (ih) (oh)

seed that with the sun's love in the Spring be-comes the Rose.
(ee) (ah) (ih) (oh)

Many different meter signatures are used in music. So far, you have read music in $\frac{2}{4}$, $\frac{3}{4}$, and $\frac{4}{4}$. The song "Winter Carol" is written in $\frac{6}{8}$ meter. In $\frac{6}{8}$, the eighth note (♪) is the beat note, and gets one count.

Preparation 5

- Form two groups to clap the eighth-note beat and the rhythm pattern.

- Clap the rhythm of the melody below. Look for the pickup note at the beginning of the melody.
- Sing the melody on syllables or numbers.

so	do'	fa	so	la		so	do'	re'	mi'
5	1'	4	5	6		5	1'	2'	3'

- Find this melody in "Winter Carol."

Preparation 6

- Sing this melody with syllables or numbers. Notice that this melody is notated in bass clef.

do	re	mi	so	fa	mi
1	2	3	5	4	3

- Find this melody in "Winter Carol." Which vocal part sings it?

Winter Carol

Words by Jane Foster Knox
Music by Mark Wilson

joy – ful car – ol we sing to night; No – el, No – el!____ Our (eh)

joy – ful car – ol we sing to night; No – el, No – el!____ Our (eh)

joy – ful car – ol we sing to night; No – el, No – el!____ Our (eh)

voic – es blend-ing in pure de–light; No – el, sing glad No – el!____ We (eh)

voic – es blend-ing in pure de–light; No – el, sing glad No – el!____ We (eh)

voic – es blend-ing in pure_ de–light; No – el, sing glad No – el!____ (eh)

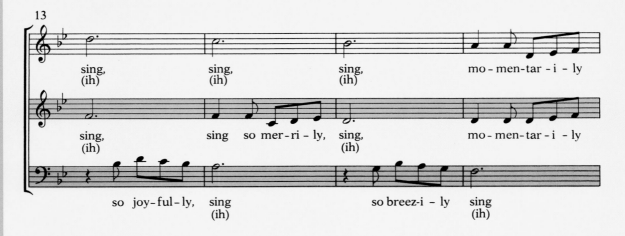

25

fa – ces glow in the can – dle light. No – el, sing glad No – el! _____
(eh)

fa – ces glow in the can – dle light. No – el, sing glad No – el! _____
(eh)

fa – ces glow in the can – dle light. No – el, sing glad No – el! _____
(eh)

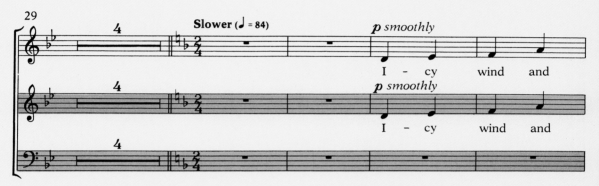

29

Slower (♩ = 84)

p smoothly

I – cy wind and

p smoothly

I – cy wind and

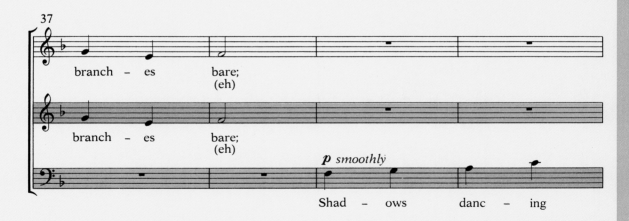

37

branch – es bare;
(eh)

branch – es bare;
(eh)

p smoothly

Shad – ows danc – ing

Moon – light, cold on ice and snow, (oh)

Moon – light, cold on ice and snow, (oh)

ev – 'ry – where. Moon – light, cold on ice and snow. (eh) (oh)

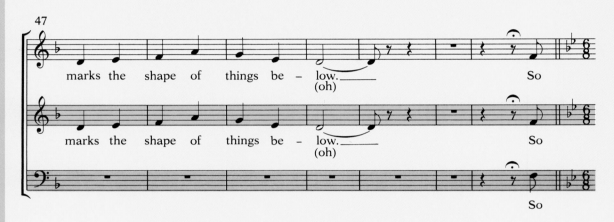

marks the shape of things be – low. (oh) So

marks the shape of things be – low. (oh) So

So

Tempo I (♩.= 100)

come a – way from the ice and snow; No – el, No – el! And (eh)

come a – way from the ice and snow; No – el, No – el! And (eh)

come a – way from the ice and snow; No – el, No – el! And (eh)

58

warm your-self by the fire's __ glow. No – el, sing glad No – el! _____ We
(eh)

warm your-self by the fire's __ glow. No – el, sing glad No – el! _____ We
(eh)

warm your-self by the fire's __ glow. No – el, sing glad No – el! _____
(eh)

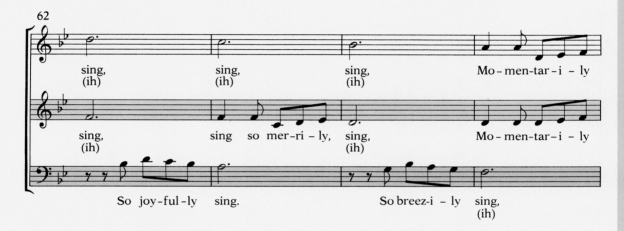

62

sing,   sing,   sing,   Mo – men-tar – i – ly
(ih)   (ih)   (ih)

sing,   sing so mer – ri – ly, sing,   Mo – men-tar – i – ly
(ih)   (ih)

So joy-ful –ly sing.   So breez-i – ly sing,
(ih)

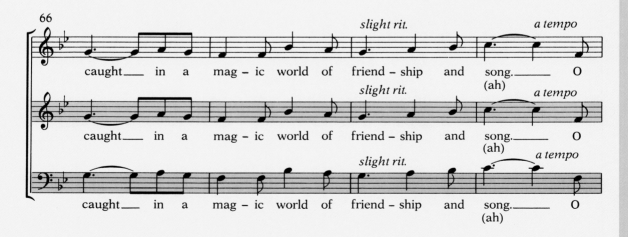

66

slight rit.   *a tempo*

caught __ in a mag – ic world of friend – ship and song. _____ O
(ah)

slight rit.   *a tempo*

caught __ in a mag – ic world of friend – ship and song. _____ O
(ah)

slight rit.   *a tempo*

caught __ in a mag – ic world of friend – ship and song. _____ O
(ah)

Preparation 7

- Count aloud as you clap each beat. Emphasize the accented beats.

The same pattern can be shown in this notation.

You have just clapped alternating groups of six beats and three beats.

group of 6   group of 3

The rhythm structure of "Praise to the Lord" is based on the same grouping.

- Perform this rhythm pattern. Use a pat-slide motion for the half notes and dotted half notes, and clap for the eighth notes.

- Sing this melody on syllables or numbers. Then form groups and sing it as a two-part round.

Praise to the Lord

M.J.

Praise,   praise to the   Lord.   Praise,
(eh)   (ah)   (eh)

praise to the   Lord._____   Praise Him with the tim-brel and the
(ah)

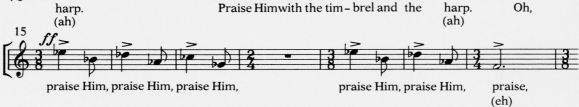

harp.   Praise Him with the tim-brel and the   harp.   Oh,
(ah)   (ah)

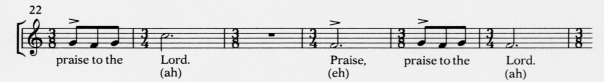

praise Him, praise Him, praise Him,   praise Him, praise Him,   praise,
(eh)

praise to the   Lord.   Praise,   praise to the   Lord.
(ah)   (eh)   (ah)

Praise Him,   praise Him,   all   ye   peo – ple;

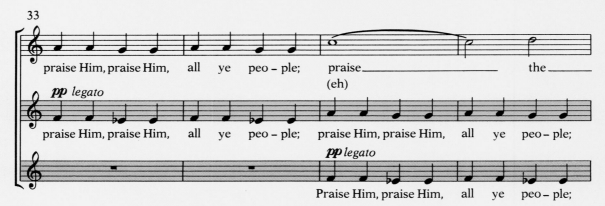

praise Him, praise Him,   all   ye   peo – ple;   praise_____ the____
(eh)

praise Him, praise Him,   all   ye   peo – ple;   praise Him, praise Him,   all   ye   peo – ple;

Praise Him, praise Him,   all   ye   peo – ple;

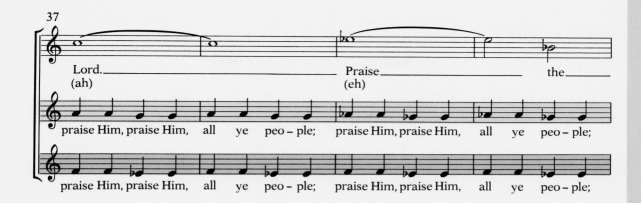

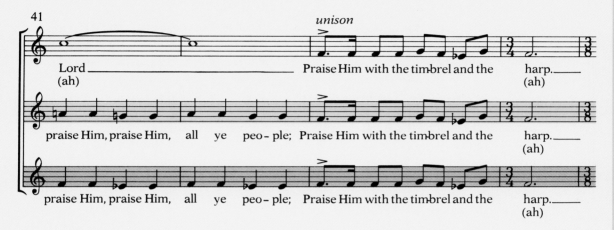

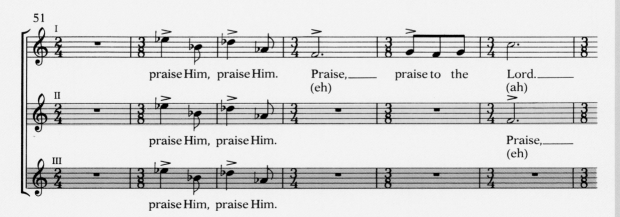

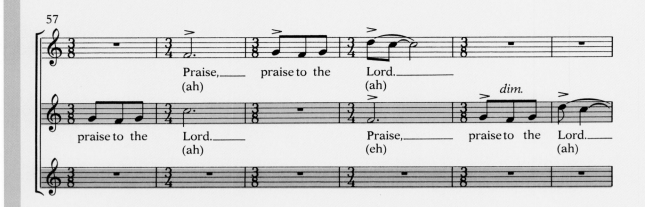

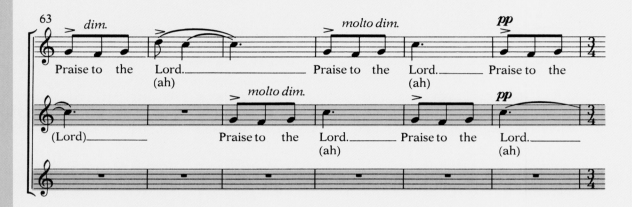

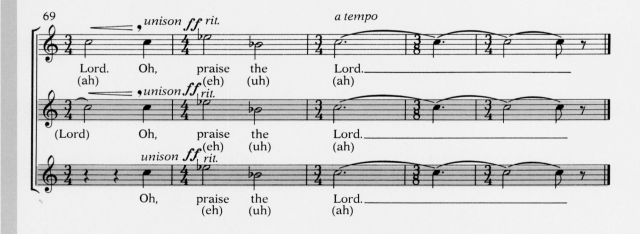

HOLIDAY SONGS

The song "Hanerot Halalu" is in minor.

Preparation 8

A **minor scale** uses the same scale tones as its **relative major scale**, but the tonal center is the sixth note of the major scale, *la₁* (6), instead of on the first note, *do* (1).

- Use the tone ladder to sing the F major scale beginning on *do* (1) and the D minor scale beginning on *la₁* (6).

Major and minor scales can be notated this way:

la₁   ti₁   do   re   mi   fa   so   la   ti   do¹

Preparation 9

- Sing this pattern to establish the tonal center for D minor.

- Sing this phrase from "Hanerot Halalu," which is in D minor.

la₁ do mi
6₁   1   3

Hanerot Halalu

Words and music by Baruch J. Cohon
Arranged by Blanche Chass

314

315

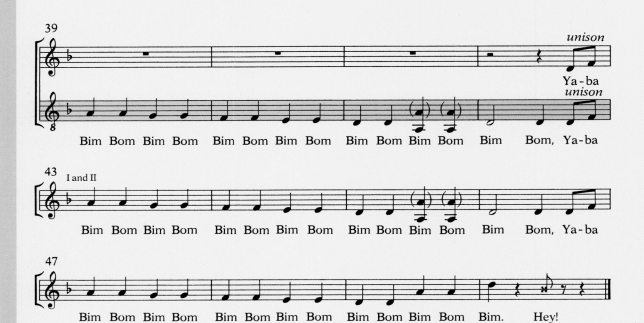

unison

Ya-ba

unison

Bim Bom Bim Bom Bim Bom Bim Bom Bim Bom Bim Bom Bim Bom, Ya-ba

I and II

Bim Bom Bim Bom Bim Bom Bim Bom Bim Bom Bim Bom Bim Bom, Ya-ba

Bim Bom Bim Bom Bim Bom Bim Bom Bim Bom Bim Bom Bim. Hey!

Preparation 10

- Perform rhythm pattern A from "This Is Christmas" by pat-sliding the half notes, patting the quarter notes, and clapping the eighth notes.

- Perform rhythm pattern B with the same body percussion. Make no sound on the rests.

- Form two groups and perform both patterns at the same time.

Preparation 11

- Sing these parts on syllables or numbers.

- Find these parts in "This Is Christmas."

317

This Is Christmas

Words by Keith W. Derrickson and Jane Foster Knox
Music by Keith W. Derrickson

319

68

for shar - ing. Christ-mas is the sea-son, the sea - son for love. It's

Eve will soon be here. Child - ren, eyes a - glow,___ it's Christ - mas! It's

fill the air, Can-dle-light shin-ing bright, this is Christ - mas! It's

72

Christ - mas!___ Re - mem - ber tid-ings of love___ and good cheer,___

Christ - mas!___ Re - mem - ber tid-ings of love___ and good cheer,___

Christ - mas!___ Re - mem - ber tid-ings of love___ and good cheer,___

76

I and II

(cheer) And spread the spi - rit of Christ - mas through all

III

(cheer) And spread the spi - rit of Christ - mas through all

80

I and II

dim. e rit. *a tempo*

the year.

III *dim. e rit.* *a tempo*

the year.___

SOME UNUSUAL VOCAL STYLES

Some twentieth-century choral music requires singers to use their
voices in unusual ways. In "Radiator Lions" you will sing, say, and
whisper the words.

Preparation 12

"Radiator Lions" contains many short spoken and sung passages.

Symbol Explanations

- Spoken
- Spoken with vocal inflection
- [W] Whisper
- [SH] Shout as LOUDLY as possible
- ∿∿∿ Continue until instructed to stop
- ⌒ Crescendo according to the rise and fall of the line

- Follow the directions for each to know when to sing, speak, or
  whisper.

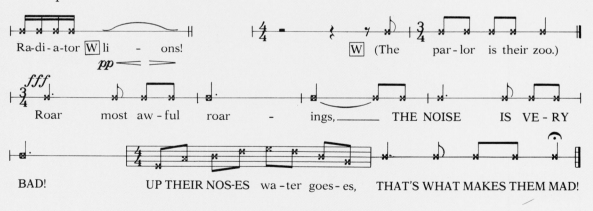

Ra-di-a-tor [W] li - ons!
pp

[W] (The par-lor is their zoo.)

fff
Roar most aw-ful roar - ings,_____ THE NOISE IS VE-RY

BAD! UP THEIR NOS-ES wa-ter goes-es, THAT'S WHAT MAKES THEM MAD!

Radiator Lions

Words by Dorothy Aldiss
Music by M.J.

li - - ons.____ But

days when it is ve - ry cold and George can't go out - doors his

par - lor pets will glow - er and crouch up - on all fours, [SH] And

I roar most aw - ful roar - ings,____ THE NOISE IS VE - RY

II roar most aw - ful SSSS ———— Sh PPSS ——— (Blow through pursed lips) ———— WHISTLE (one pitch)

BAD! UP THEIR NOS - ES wa - ter goes - es, THAT'S WHAT MAKES THEM MAD!

I and II But George loves ra - di - a - tor li - ons. He's

glad, al - though they're wild,_ he hasn't dogs or pol-i - wogs like

an - - y oth - er child.

CHORAL BLEND

Remember that one characteristic of good choral singing is blend. Blending your voice with those of the other singers creates a unified sound. Focus on making a smooth sound as you sing *Sanctus*.

Preparation 13

Sanctus requires you to sing in a very sustained style, with smooth changes between chords.

- Listen to *Sanctus* for the chord sounds most often used.
- Sing the three main chords used in *Sanctus* on pitch numbers.

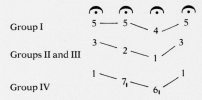

In *Sanctus* these chords are notated like this.

325

Sanctus

Franz Schubert (1797–1828)

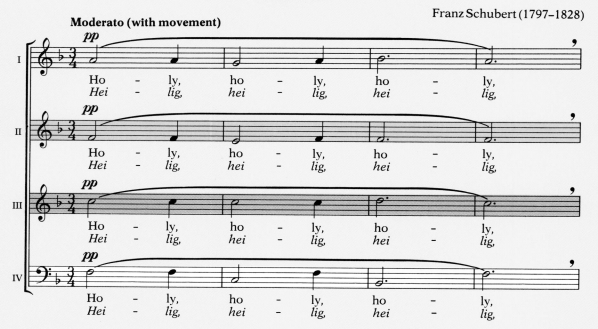

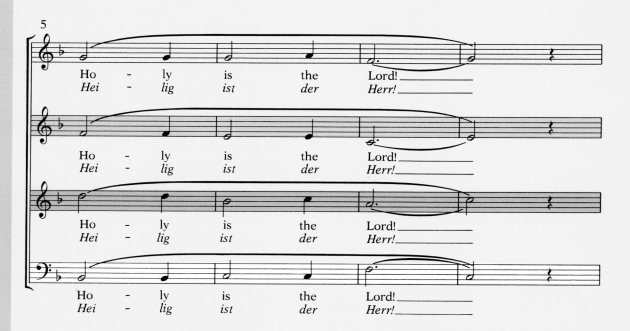

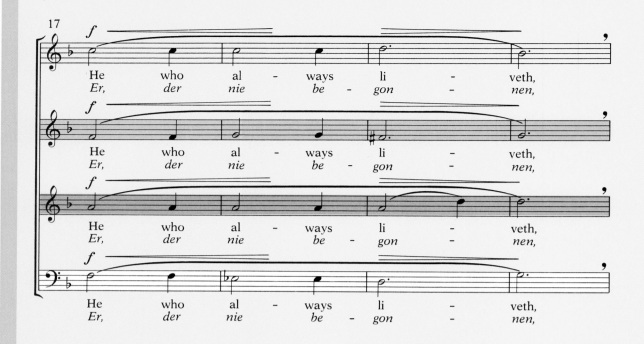

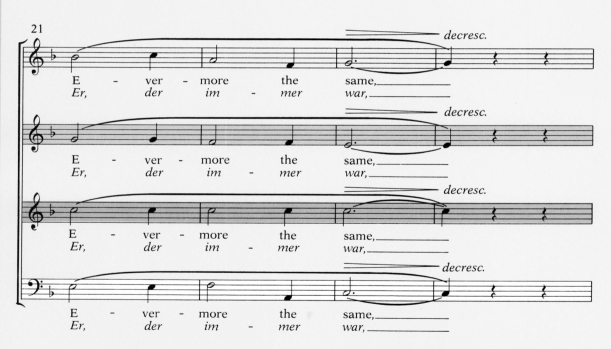

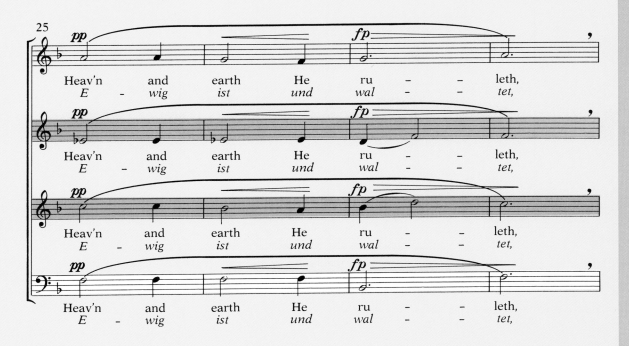

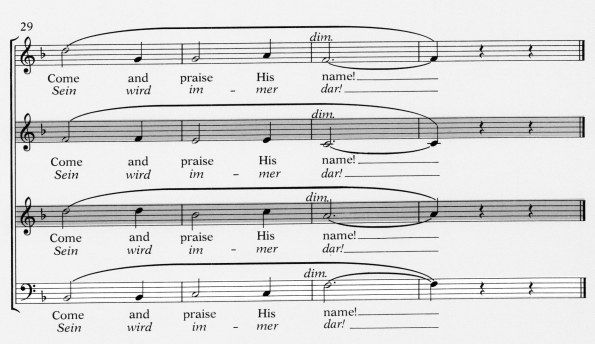

Preparation 14

- Perform this syncopated rhythm pattern from "The Promised Land" by patting the quarter notes and clapping the eighth notes.

- Sing this melody. Look for the pickup note.

On Jor-dan's storm - y banks I stand_ and cast a wist - ful eye

The *8* below the treble clef in Part I means you should sing one octave lower than the music is written.

The Promised Land

Pioneer hymn
Arr. by Carl J. Nygard, Jr.

On Jor-dan's storm - y banks I stand__ and

cast a wist - ful eye Ca - naan's fair and_ hap - py land_ where

cast a wist - ful eye To__ Ca - naan's fair and_ hap - py land_ where

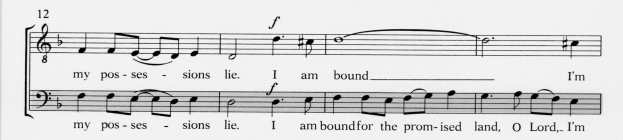

my pos - ses - sions lie. I am bound_____ I'm

my pos - ses - sions lie. I am bound for the prom - ised land, O Lord,_ I'm

331

who will___ come and go with me? I am bound for the prom - ised

who will___ come and go with me? I am bound for the prom - ised

land.   *p much slower* Soon will the Lord___ pre -

land.   *p much slower* Soon will the Lord pre -

pare my soul for joys be - yond___ the skies, *f* *a tempo* Where___ nev - er - end - ing

pare my soul for joys be - yond___ the skies, *f* *a tempo* Where nev - er - end - ing

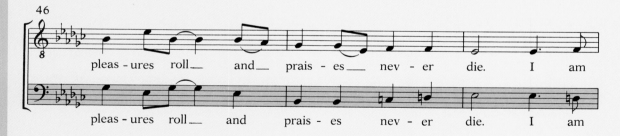

pleas - ures roll___ and___ prais - es___ nev - er die. I am

pleas - ures roll___ and prais - es nev - er die. I am

bound for the prom - ised land, O Lord, I'm bound for the prom - ised

bound,   O Lord, I'm   bound_____

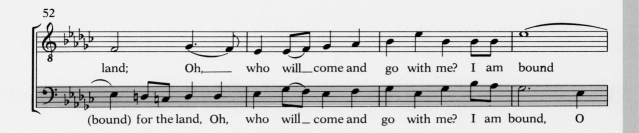

land; Oh,_____ who will_come and go with me? I am bound

(bound) for the land, Oh, who will_come and go with me? I am bound, O

(bound)_____ for the prom-ised_____

Lord, I'm bound,_____ Yes, I'm head-ed for the prom-ised_____

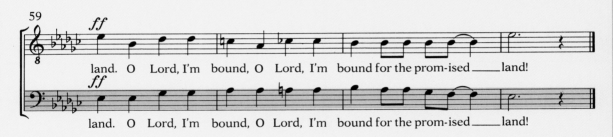

ff

land. O Lord, I'm bound, O Lord, I'm bound for the prom-ised_____land!

ff

land. O Lord, I'm bound, O Lord, I'm bound for the prom-ised_____land!

To the Morning

Words and music by Dan Fogelberg
Arr. by D. H. Arthur

I, II and III
Moderato   8   **A** *unison*

Watch-ing the sun, watch-ing it come, watch-ing it come up o - ver the

11

roof — — tops   Cloud-y and warm, may-be a

14

I   *mp*   *divisi*

storm,   you can   nev - er quite tell from the   morn — — ing, And it's

II and III *mp*   *divisi*

storm,   you can   nev - er quite tell from the   morn — — ing, And it's

44

sea - sons, and may - be _____ they change, _____ and

sea - sons, and may - be _____ they change, _____ and

47 I *rit.*   *mp*   *freely*

may - be _____ true love _____ is not so strange.

II *rit.*   *mp*   *freely*

may - be _____ true love _____ is not so strange.

III *rit.*   *mp*   *freely*

may - be _____ true love _____ is not so strange.

51   2 F   *a tempo* *legato*

Ooh _____

a tempo *legato*

Ooh _____

a tempo *legato*

Ooh _____

57 I G

The suns of the day, _ now they hur-ry a - way, _ now they are gone _ un - til to -

II and III

The suns of the day, _ now they hu-rry a - way, _ now they are gone un - til to -

337

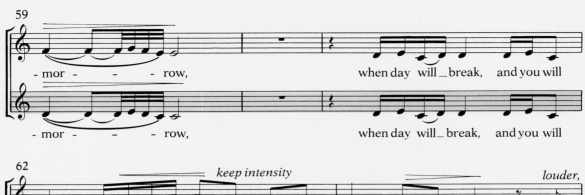

-mor - - - row, when day will _ break, and you will

-mor - - - row, when day will _ break, and you will

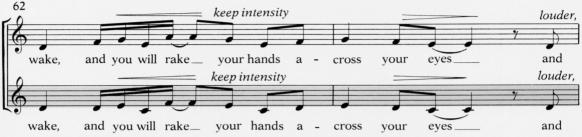

keep intensity *louder,*

wake, and you will rake _ your hands a - cross your eyes _____ and

keep intensity *louder,*

wake, and you will rake _ your hands a - cross your eyes _____ and

with great intensity D.S. al Coda ⊕ **11**

re - al - ize that it's

with great intensity D.S. al Coda ⊕ **11**

re - al - ize that it's

Preparation 16

Like "Praise to the Lord" and "Radiator Lions," "Chartless" has changing meters.

- Form two groups to tap the steady beat and the rhythm pattern.

- Sing these melodies separately, then form two groups and sing them together.

Preparation 17

The middle section of "Chartless" requires the singers to perform the same melody, but to begin at different times.

- Learn to sing this melody. It has no meter signature. Follow the rhythm of the words as you sing.

I nev - er spoke with God,_____ Nor vis - it - ed in heav'n_____

- Perform this melody. Each person should begin at a different time.

Chartless

Words by Emily Dickinson
Music by C. M. Shearer

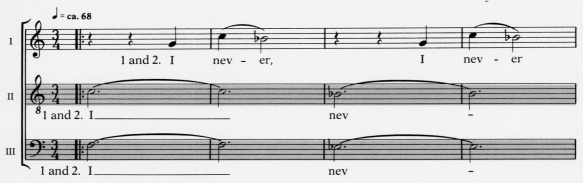

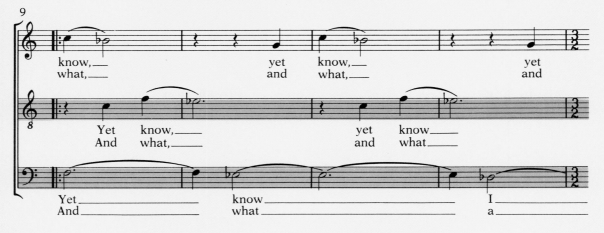

know I how a heath-er looks, And be. I nev-er spoke with God,
what a wave must

yet know I how a heath-er looks, must be. I nev-er
and what a wave

(I) how heath - er looks,
(a) wave must be.

Nor vis-it-ed in heav'n;

spoke with God, Nor vis-it-ed in heav'n;

I nev-er spoke with God, Nor vis-it-ed in heav'n;

Tempo I

Yet cer - tain am I of the

Yet cer - tain am I of the

Yet cer - tain am I of the

I know.
solo or soli
spot As if the chart were giv - en.
choir

spot As if the chart were giv - en.

spot As if the chart were giv - en.

*Each singer begins independently, singing each syllable at about ♩=128. After singing both lines of poetry twice, singers should hold the gathering note (⬭) until the last voice finishes singing "heav'n."

341

Preparation 18

The words *sing me home* are repeated throughout this song, but with different melodies and in different voice parts.

● Practice saying the words in rhythm, then singing the different sounds of the same phrase below.

Which examples are similar? Which are contrasting?

Sing Me Home

Words and music by Carl J. Nygard, Jr.

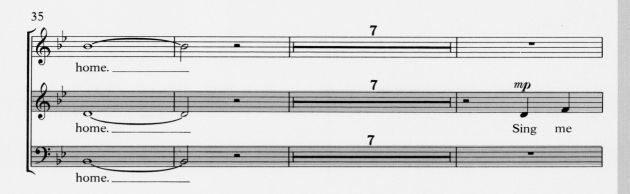

song, Let the song ____ sing me home. _____ Sing me

Let the song sing me home. _____ Sing me

song, Let the song sing me home. _____ Sing me

home through the day, ____ sing me home through the night.

home, _____ sing me home. _____ Sing me

home through the day, sing me home through the night. Sing me

Sing me home. Sing me home, sing me

home, _____ sing ____ me home. _____ Sing me

home, _____ sing me home. _____

home now to stay, ____ through the dark, through the light.

home, _____ sing me home, _____

sub. **p**

Sing me home, through the dark, through the light. Sing me

Sing me home sing __ me home. _____

Sing me home, sing me home. ___

home, _____ sing me home. ___

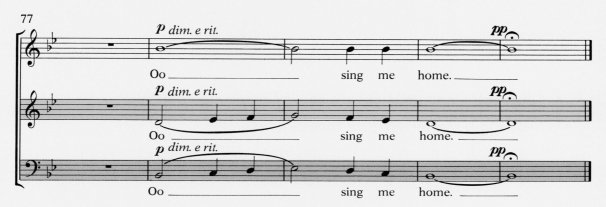

Oo _____ sing me home. ___

Oo _____ sing me home. ___

Oo _____ sing me home. ___

Preparation 19

- Clap this pattern.

Remember that a half note (𝅗𝅥) usually lasts for two beats. Now substitute three evenly spaced quarter notes (), called a **quarter-note triplet**, for the half note.

- Clap the new pattern.

- Find the quarter-note triplets in "Dream a Dream."
- Clap this pattern with the quarter-note triplet, then say the words in rhythm.

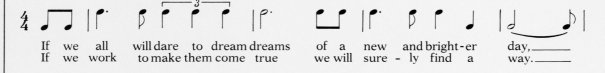

If   we   all   will dare to dream dreams   of   a   new   and bright-er   day,_____
If   we work   to make them come   true   we will sure – ly find   a   way._____

Preparation 20

Long, flowing phrases give this song a beautiful effect. The pattern in Preparation 19 should be sung on one sustained breath. Here is the same pattern with pitches added.

- Sing Part I in unison. Then form groups and sing both parts as you work for in-tune singing and smooth phrases.

Dream a Dream

Words and music by Ed Robertson

349

Preparation 21

- Count and clap this rhythm pattern from "Chichester Prayer."

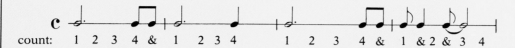

count: 1 2 3 4 & 1 2 3 4   1 2 3 4 & 1 & 2 & 3 4

- Now count and tap this pattern.

count: 1 2 3 4   1 2 & 3 4   1 2 3 4   1 & 2 & 3 4

The two patterns look like this when they are combined. Try them together.

In "Chichester Prayer," this combination of one voice following the other first occurs in measures 16 through 19.

- Clap measures 16–19 in rhythm, say the words in rhythm, and then add the pitches.
- Find other places in the music where similar patterns follow one another in the voices.

Preparation 22

- Clap these parts. Then form groups and clap them together.
- Read the words in rhythm, then add the pitches.

I (pray)___   To love more dear - ly___   Each day
  do fa
  1 4

II (pray)___   To see more clear - ly___   To fol-low more near - ly___
   do fa
   1 4

How are the two vocal parts similar and different?

352

Chichester Prayer

Words attributed to Richard of Chichester
Music by Carl J. Nygard, Jr.

ADDITIONAL ROUNDS FOR SIGHT READING

Preparation 23

- Listen to "Alleluia I." How many phrases do you hear? How are they different?
- Sing this pattern. Which phrase does it sound most like?

- Compare this pattern with the first phrase of "Alleluia I." How are they different?
- Sing the entire round on pitch syllables or numbers.

Alleluia I

Anonymous

Al – le – lu – ia, al – le – lu – ia.

A – – – men, a – – – men.

Preparation 24

- Sing this triad pattern. This pattern contains C, E, G, C', the pitches in the C major chord.

Both "Alleluia II" and "Jubilate" are based on this C major triad. Warming up with these sounds will help you sense the tonal center of both rounds.

- Find these pitches in "Alleluia II" and "Jubilate."
- Sing "Alleluia II" on pitch syllables or numbers.

Preparation 25

- Form two groups to perform the steady beat and the uneven rhythm pattern.

- Find this pattern in "Jubilate."
- Tap all the rhythms in "Jubilate," then sing the round on pitch syllables.
- When you have learned both rounds, try writing new words to each.

Alleluia II

Anonymous

Al - le - lu - ia, al - le - lu - ia, al - le - lu - ia, al - le - lu - ia.

Jubilate

Michael Praetorius (1571–1621)

Ju - bi - la -te De - o, ju - bi - la - te De - o, al - le - lu - ia.

O Music, Sweet Music

Words and music by Lowell Mason

O — mu – sic, sweet mu – sic, thy— prais-es we will sing, We—
will— tell of the— plea - sure and— hap - pi -ness you— bring.
Mu – sic, mu - sic, let the cho - rus ring!

Preparation 27

- Play or tap this pattern.

- Say the pattern in rhythm using "la."

Fa - la - la - la - la - la - la - la - la - la - la,   joy - ful- ly

- Find all the places in the "Mystery Tune" where this pattern appears. Practice singing it with pitch syllables or numbers. Work for a smooth choral blend in all voices.

Preparation 28

In measure 34 of this round, the meter changes from $\frac{6}{8}$ to $\frac{2}{4}$. Since both $\frac{6}{8}$ and $\frac{2}{4}$ have two beats to a measure, the beat stays constant when you change to the new meter.

- Tap the steady beat as you say the rhythm using "la." Keep the feeling of 2 when you come to the $\frac{2}{4}$ section. This will help you make a smooth change.

Mystery Tune

Traditional German round
Arr. M.J.

TIME LINE

Michael Praetorius 1571–1621

1600

1620 Mayflower lands at Plymouth Rock

Jean Baptiste Lully 1632–1687

1643 Louis XIV becomes king of France at age 5

1650

Johann Pachelbel 1653–1706
Henry Purcell 1659–1695

1666 Newton discovers Law of Gravity

Antonio Vivaldi 1678–1741

Johann Sebastian Bach 1685–1750
George Frederick Handel 1685–1759

1700

Franz Joseph Haydn 1732–1809
John Stafford Smith 1750–1836

1750

Wolfgang Amadeus Mozart 1756–1791

1769 James Watt patents his steam engine

Ludwig van Beethoven 1770–1827

1775

1775 American Revolution (ended 1783)
1776 American Declaration of Independence

Francis Scott Key 1779–1843

1787 American Constitutional Convention
1788 John Fitch invents steamboat
1789 French Revolution; George Washington first
president of United States
1791 Bill of Rights
1793 Eli Whitney invents the cotton gin

Franz Schubert 1797–1828

1800

1803 Louisiana Purchase
1804 Napoleon crowned emperor; Lewis and Clark
expedition

Fanny Mendelssohn Hensel 1805–1847

1807 Robert Fulton builds first commercial
steamboat; London streets lighted by gas

Felix Mendelssohn 1809–1847
Frédéric Chopin 1810–1849
Robert Schumann 1810–1856

1812 War of 1812

Richard Wagner 1813–1883

1815 Napoleon defeated in Battle of Waterloo

1819 First steamship crosses Atlantic

1825 Opening of the Erie Canal
1825 First public railroad opened in England

1825

Johannes Brahms 1833–1897

Georges Bizet 1838–1875

1838 Daguerre takes first photographs

Modest Mussorgsky 1839–1881
Peter Ilyich Tchaikovsky 1840–1893

Edvard Grieg 1843–1907
Nicolai Rimsky-Korsakov 1844–1908

1844 First telegraph message transmitted

1846 First use of ether as an anesthetic

1848 California Gold Rush; first Women's Rights
Convention

361

1850

John Philip Sousa 1854–1932

Cécile Chaminade 1857–1944
Giacomo Puccini 1858–1924

Claude Debussy 1862–1918

Scott Joplin 1868–1917

James Weldon Johnson 1871–1938
Ralph Vaughan Williams 1872–1958
W.C. (William Christopher) Handy 1873–1958
Arnold Schoenberg 1874–1951
Charles Ives 1874–1954
Robert Frost 1874–1963

1875

Igor Stravinsky 1882–1971

Ferdinand ("Jelly Roll") Morton 1885–1941
Gertrude ("Ma") Rainey 1886–1939
Ernst Toch 1887–1964
T.S. (Thomas Stearns) Eliot 1888–1965

Sergei Prokofiev 1891–1953

Bessie Smith 1894–1937
William Grant Still 1895–1978

George Gershwin 1898–1937

1900

Louis Armstrong 1900–1971
Harry Partch 1901–1974
Langston Hughes 1902–1967
Ogden Nash 1902–1971

Milt Hinton 1910–

John Cage 1912–
Morton Gould 1913–
Benjamin Britten 1913–1976

Milton Babbitt 1916–
Eve Merriam 1916–
Lou Harrison 1917–
Leonard Bernstein 1918–

1860 Civil War (ended 1865)
1863 Gettysburg Address; Emancipation Proclamation
1865 Abraham Lincoln assassinated

1869 First American transcontinental railroad

1876 Alexander Graham Bell invents telephone
1877 Thomas Edison invents the phonograph

1879 Edison invents improved incandescent electric light bulb

1885 Louis Pasteur develops milk "pasteurization"
1886 Statue of Liberty unveiled in New York Harbor

1895 Wilhelm Roentgen discovers X-rays

1898 Spanish-American War

1901 Guglielmo Marconi transmits wireless telegraph signals across Atlantic
1902 Pierre and Marie Curie discover radium
1903 Wilbur and Orville Wright make first successful airplane flight
1904 First sound moving picture
1905 Albert Einstein offers Theory of Relativity
1906 San Francisco earthquake and fire

1908 Model T Ford produced
1909 Robert Peary and Matthew Henson reach North Pole
1910 Discovery of the South Pole; discovery of protons and electrons

1912 *Titanic* disaster

1914 Opening of the Panama Canal; World War I (ended 1918)

1917 Russian Revolution

People	Historical Events
Dave Brubeck 1920–	1920 First commercial radio broadcast; suffrage (19th Amendment)
Katsutoshi Nagasawa 1923– **Paul Desmond** 1924–1977 **Pierre Boulez** 1925–	

1925

	1927 Charles Lindbergh's flight across the Atlantic; first television transmission
Burt Bacharach 1928–	1928 Sir Alexander Fleming discovers penicillin
	1929 New York stock market crash; beginning of worldwide depression
Claude Bolling 1930– **Stephen Sondheim** 1930–	
Shel Silverstein 1932– **Isao Tomita** 1932– **John Williams** 1932– **Krzysztof Penderecki** 1933–	1933 Nazi Revolution in Germany
Terry Riley 1935–	
Philip Glass 1937– **Gordon Lightfoot** 1938–	1939 World War II (ended 1945)
Trevor Nunn 1940–	
David Fanshawe 1942– **George Harrison** 1943– **Vangelis** 1943–	
Andrew Lloyd Webber 1948– **Stephen Schwartz** 1948– **Rick Springfield** 1949–	

1950

	1950 Vietnam War (ended 1975)
	1957 Launching of *Sputnik,* first earth satellite
	1961 First successful manned orbital space flight
	1962 Cuban missile crisis
	1963 President John F. Kennedy assassinated
	1965 First "walk" outside spaceship by an astronaut
	1968 Martin Luther King, Jr., and Robert F. Kennedy assassinated
	1969 First men land on the moon
	1971 Voting age lowered to 18 years

1975

	1976 U.S. celebrates its bicentennial on July 4; Viking I and II landers set down on Mars
	1981 Sandra Day O'Connor becomes first woman appointed to the Supreme Court; first reusable spacecraft, space shuttle *Columbia,* travels into space and returns to earth
	1983 Sally Ride becomes the first American woman to travel in space
	1984 First mechanical heart implanted in a human
	1985 Worldwide Live Aid concert to benefit famine victims in Ethiopia
	1986 Statue of Liberty centennial celebration; Hands Across America, nationwide joining of hands to benefit the homeless in America
	1987 *Voyager* makes first nonstop flight around the world without refueling

363

GLOSSARY

ABA form a three-part form in which there is repetition after contrast, 21

AB form the organization of a composition into two different sections, 3

accent (>) placement of emphasis or stress on certain beats, 3

art song music written for solo voice and instrumental accompaniment, usually keyboard, 111

atonal music music characterized by the absence of a tonal center and equal emphasis on all twelve tones of the chromatic scale, 92

ballad a song that tells a story, 130

bar lines lines separating measures, 18

baroque style the common musical characteristics reflected by the music composed between 1600 and 1750, 17

bitonality harmony created by playing two different tonalities at the same time, 108

blues a melancholy style of American music characterized by flatted notes and a syncopated, often slow jazz rhythm, 104

calypso style folk-style music from the Caribbean Islands, 10

canon a form of music in which different vocal or instrumental parts take up the melody, successively creating harmony, 82

changing meter a combination of various meters, 48

chord three or more pitches sounding together, 4

classical style the common musical characteristics reflected by the music composed between 1750 and 1830, 17

coda concluding section, 20

compound meter meter whose beat can be subdivided into threes and/or sixes, 61

consonance the sounding of a combination of tones that produces little tension, 80

crescendo getting louder, 13

decrescendo getting softer, 13

development the expanded treatment of a musical idea, 147

dissonance the sounding of a combination of pitches that create harmonic tension and sound incomplete, 108

dominant chord a chord built on the fifth tone of a scale, 11

dotted quarter note the basic beat in compound meter, 60

duple beats grouped into sets of two, 18

dynamics levels of loudness and softness, 13

eighth note (♪) a symbol for a sound in music that is one-eighth as long as the sound of a whole note, 8

eighth rest (𝄾) a symbol for an interval of silence between tones lasting as long as an eighth note, 8

expressionism a movement in the arts characterized by the artist's concern with the expression of feelings about an object or event rather than realistically depicting the object itself, 93

forte (*f*) loud, **13**

found objects sources of tone color that are ordinary items that wouldn't usually be thought of as musical instruments, **181**

free form a composition that changes from one performance to the next, **158**

half note (♩) a symbol for a sound in music that is one half as long as the sound of a whole note, **4**

harmony a musical combination of tones or chords, **80**

home tone the focus or tonal center of a scale, or system of tones, **80**

homophonic music having one melodic line with the other parts providing harmony, **83**

irregular meter a mixture of duple and triple meters in a repeating pattern, **48**

jazz a style of American music originated in the South by black Americans. It is characterized by strong, prominent meter, improvisation, and dotted or syncopated rhythms, **52**

key scale or system of tones in which all the notes have a definite relationship to, and are based on, the tonal center or keynote, **100**

key tone the focus or tonal center of a scale or system of tones, **11**

legato music that sounds smooth, **141**

major chord a chord that consists of the first, third, and fifth notes of a major scale, **25**

measures groups of beats, **18**

meter the organization of beats into recurring sets, **18**

minor chord a chord that consists of the first, lowered third, and fifth notes of a major scale, **25**

modulation transition from a section of music based on one key to a section based on a different key, **100**

monophonic music having a single melodic line with no accompaniment, **83**

motive a short musical unit that keeps its basic identity through many repetitions, **127**

natural (♮) symbol indicating that a sharp or a flat should be cancelled, **25**

Ondes Martenot a precursor to the present-day synthesizer, **178**

oratorio a dramatic musical composition usually set to a religious text and performed by solo voices, chorus, and orchestra, without action, special costumes, or scenery, **83**

ostinato continuous repeating of a passage, **54**

phrases the building blocks of form, **120**

piano (*p*) soft, **13**

pipe organ keyboard instrument whose sound is produced by wind moving through pipes, **172**

pizzicato music played by plucking the strings of a stringed instrument with the finger instead of bowing the strings, **106**

polyphonic music having two or more independent melodic parts sounding together, **83**

polyrhythm a combination of two or more different rhythm patterns played at the same time, **70**

polytonality a combination of two or more tonalities (keys) played at the same time, **108**

prepared piano piano that has been altered by items of wood, metal, rubber, etc., placed between the strings of the piano, 175

program music a composition whose title or accompanying remarks link it with a story, idea, or emotion, 50

quadruple meter beats that are grouped into sets of four, 40

quarter note (♩) a symbol for a sound in music that is one fourth as long as the sound of a whole note, 3

quarter rest (𝄽) a symbol for an interval of silence between tones lasting as long as a quarter note, 3

reggae style popular music from the Caribbean Islands, 5

register the range of a voice or instrument, 102

Renaissance style the common musical characteristics reflected by the music composed between 1450 and 1600, 17

retrograde a melody that is performed backwards, 88

rhythm pattern a combination of long and short sounds which is repeated, 3

ritardando gradual slowing of the tempo, 20

romantic style the common musical characteristics reflected by the music composed between 1830 and 1900, 17

root the lowest pitch of each chord, 11

salsa a style of Latin dance music originating in Cuba. It is characterized by exciting rhythm and jazz and blues styles and harmonies, 70

serial music atonal music written using a technique based on the successive repetition of all twelve tones of the chromatic scale in a fixed order, 90

simple meter meter whose beat can be divided into twos and/or fours, 40

sonata allegro a musical form that uses the overall design of exposition, development, and recapitulation, 149

staccato music that sounds crisp and detached, 141

steady beat the underlying beat or pulse, 3

steel drums "homemade" percussion instruments found in the West Indies, 182

strophic form form in which the music is repeated with each new verse or stanza of text, 130

style quality that is characteristic of a culture, individual, or historical period, 2

subdominant chord chord based on the fourth tone of the scale, 104

symphony long orchestral work organized into three to five movements, 149

syncopation rhythm pattern that has unexpected sounds and silences, 10

synthesizer an instrument for producing electronic music that combines sound generators and modifiers in a single control system, 179

synth-pop popular music that uses synthesized tone color, 30

tempo the speed of the beat, 8

ternary form (ABA) a three-part form in which there is repetition after contrast, 21

texture the character of the different layers of sound in music, 83

Theremin first electronic musical instrument, invented by and named for Leon Theremin, 178

tonality the relation of melodic and harmonic elements between the tones of any major or minor scale to the home tone, 80

tone color the unique sound of each instrument or voice, 13

tone row a type of pitch organization made up of all twelve tones of the chromatic scale that has no tonal center and in which all pitches are equal, 90

tonic chord a chord built on the first tone or key tone of a scale, 11

triple meter beats grouped into sets of three, 18

twelve-bar blues chord pattern often used in blues music based on the I, IV, and V chords, 104

twentieth-century style the common musical characteristics reflected by the music composed since 1900, 17

whole note (o) a symbol that represents a sound that lasts for four beats in meter, 4

LISTENING SELECTIONS

"A Marvelous Place," Traditional; M.J., **158**

African Sanctus by David Fanshawe, **7**

Afro-American Symphony, First Movement by William Grant Still, **106**

"Alpha" from *Albedo 39* by Vangelis, **173**

"America," Version 1, **108**

"America," Version 2, **108**

"Bachi" by Claire Fisher, **70**

Beethoven Seventh Motive Montage, **141**

Begleitungsmusik zu einer Lichtspielscene (excerpt), Op. 34, by Arnold Schoenberg, **93**

"The Birth of Kijé" by Sergei Prokofiev, **204**

Bwala, Traditional Ugandan, **6**

Canon by Johann Pachelbel, **81**

"Caprice" from Suite for Violin and Jazz Piano by Claude Bolling, **69**

"Careless Whisper" by George Michael and Andrew Ridgeley, **121**

Cedo (Gambia), **217**

Chemutengure (Zimbabwe), **218**

Classical Symphony, First Movement by Sergei Prokofiev, **150**

"Come on Baby Dance with Me" performed by Shakti, **212**

Composition for Synthesizer by Milton Babbitt, **180**

Compound Meter Montage, **68**

Concerto in D Major for Guitar and Orchestra, Third Movement by Antonio Vivaldi, **254**

Concertino for Flute and Orchestra by Cécile Chaminade, **102**

"Dream of Dreams" by Joe Sample, **234**

"Elements" by Black Uhuru, **2**

Ensembles for Synthesizer by Milton Babbitt, **173**

"The Erlking" by Franz Schubert, **111**

Étude in E Minor, Op. 25, No. 5 by Frédéric Chopin, **199**

"Ev'ry Time I Feel the Spirit" arranged by William Dawson, **207**

"Farandole" from *L'Arlésienne* Suite No. 2 by Georges Bizet, **24**

"Floe" from *Glassworks*, by Philip Glass, **127**

"Hallelujah" chorus from *Messiah* by George Frederick Handel, **84**

"Harmonic Repetition Montage," **234**

Harry Partch on *Spoils of War*, **183**

"Head over Heels" by Curt Smith and Roland Orzabal, **32**

"Hear Me Talking to You" by Ma Rainey, **104**

Heaven and Hell, Part 2 by Vangelis, **166**

"Hickory Hollow," **255**

"Historical Style Montage" ("Ode to Joy" by Beethoven), **16**

Hudan Mas (Indonesia), **226**

Infernal Dance from *The Firebird* by Igor Stravinsky, **200**

Kelefa ba (Gambia), **216**

🔘 *Kogoklaras* by Vincent McDermott, **211**

🔘 *Kondawele* (excerpt), **215**

🔘 Kyrie from Mass in G Minor by Ralph Vaughan Williams, **6**

🔘 *Madhu Kauns* (India), **213**

🔘 "Marche" by Jean Baptiste Lully, **18**

🔘 "Meter Identification Montage," **41**

🔘 "Mix 'Em Up," **44**

🔘 "Music in Fours," **40**

🔘 "Music in Threes," **40**

🔘 "Music in Twos," **40**

🔘 *O Care, thou wilt despatch me* by Thomas Weelkes, **190**

🔘 *"Pagodes"* by Claude Debussy, **228**

🔘 *The Perilous Night* by John Cage, **175**

🔘 Polyrhythm Montage, **72**

🔘 Program Music Example, **152**

🔘 "Promenade" from *Pictures at an Exhibition* by Modest Mussorgsky, **51**

🔘 "Promenade Montage," **179**

🔘 Quintet for Clarinet and Strings in A Major, K. 581, Fourth Movement by Wolfgang Amadeus Mozart, **194**

🔘 *Saint Luke Passion* by Krzysztof Penderecki, **171**

🔘 *Sambaso* (Japan), **222**

🔘 *Satto* by Katsutoshi Nagasawa, **12**

🔘 *"Schwanenlied"* by Fanny Mendelssohn Hensel, **134**

🔘 "Spring" (First Movement) from *The Four Seasons* by Antonio Vivaldi, **193**

🔘 Steel Band Music, Traditional West Indian, **182**

🔘 "Style Montage," **2**

🔘 "Suite for Percussion" by Lou Harrison, **181**

🔘 Symphony No. 7, Second Movement by Ludwig van Beethoven, **142**

🔘 *Take Five* by Paul Desmond, **49**

🔘 *Take Five* pattern, **48**

🔘 *Taksim in Mode Segah* (Turkey), **220**

🔘 "Three-Chord Strut," **120**

🔘 Toccata and Fugue in D Minor by Johann Sebastian Bach, **172**

🔘 "Tone Color Montage," **164**

🔘 "Tonight" quintet from *West Side Story* by Leonard Bernstein and Stephen Sondheim, **203**

🔘 "Twelve-Bar Blues" by Michael Treni, **235**

🔘 "Two-Chord Strut," **120**

🔘 *"Un bel dì vedremo"* from *Madama Butterfly* by Giacomo Puccini, **196**

🔘 *Unsquare Dance* by Dave Brubeck, **54**

🔘 *Variations on "America"* by Charles Ives, **109**

🔘 "The Wedding of Kijé" by Sergei Prokofiev, **205**

🔘 *Wellington's Victory* by Ludwig van Beethoven, **154**

🔘 *Wellington's Victory* Theme Montage, **153**

🔘 "The Wreck of the Edmund Fitzgerald" by Gordon Lightfoot, **130**

ALPHABETICAL SONG INDEX

A
Ahrirang, **82**
Alleluia I, **355**
Alleluia II, **356**
America, **147, 280**
April Weather, **297**

C
Chartless, **340**
Chichester Prayer, **353**
Climbing Up to Zion, **98**

D
Dream a Dream, **349**
Drunken Sailor, **261**

F
Follow the Drinkin' Gourd, **271**

G
Ghost Ship, The, **272**

H
Hanerot Halalu, **314**
Head over Heels, **35**

I
I'm Goin' Home on a Cloud, **284**

J
Joyfully Sing, **67, 359**
Jubilate, **356**

L
(Life Is a) Celebration, **123**
Love Song, **46**

M
Mama Don't 'Low, **252, 263**
Memory, **64**
Mi Caballo Blanco, **100**
Misty, Moisty Morning, **170**

O
O Music, Sweet Music, **357**
Our World, **28**
Over the Sea to Skye, **286**

P
Praise to the Lord, **310**
Promised Land, The, **330**

R
Radiator Lions, **323**
Rhythm of Life, The, **291**
River, **78, 274**
Rose, The, **299**
Run Joe, **10**

S
Samiotissa, **55**
Sanctus, **326**
Sing Me Home, **343**

T
That's What Friends Are For, **42**
This Is Christmas, **318**
To the Morning, **334**

W
Wabash Cannonball, The, **265**
Web, The, **91**
Winter Carol, **303**
Worried Man Blues, **269**
Wreck of the Edmund Fitzgerald, The, **131, 267**

CLASSIFIED INDEX

Folk Songs

African American
Ev'ry Time I Feel the Spirit, **207**
Follow the Drinkin' Gourd, **271**
I'm Goin' Home on a Cloud, **284**

American. See also *African American*
Drunken Sailor, **261**
Mama Don't 'Low, **252, 263**
Wabash Cannonball, The, **265**
Worried Man Blues, **269**

German
Joyfully Sing, **67, 359**

Greek
Samiotissa, **55**

Korean
Ahrirang, **82**

Holiday Songs and Special Days
December
Hanerot Halalu, **314**
This Is Christmas, **318**
Winter Carol, **303**

Patriotic
America, **147, 280**
Dream a Dream, **349**

Musicals, Songs from Broadway
Love Song, **46**
Memory, **64**

Poems
Backward Bill, **87**
Bravado, **15**
Cheers, **60**
Dreams, **15**
Rainbow Writing, **14**
Weather, **73**

Popular Songs
Head over Heels, **35**
(Life Is a) Celebration, **123**
Rhythm of Life, The, **291**
River, **78, 274**
Rose, The, **299**
That's What Friends Are For, **42**
To the Morning, **334**

I don't want to have to start over again in a new school. I would rather go back to my friends and my mom. There I would have to change a little - just a new school, but there I know all my friends and don't have to make new ones.